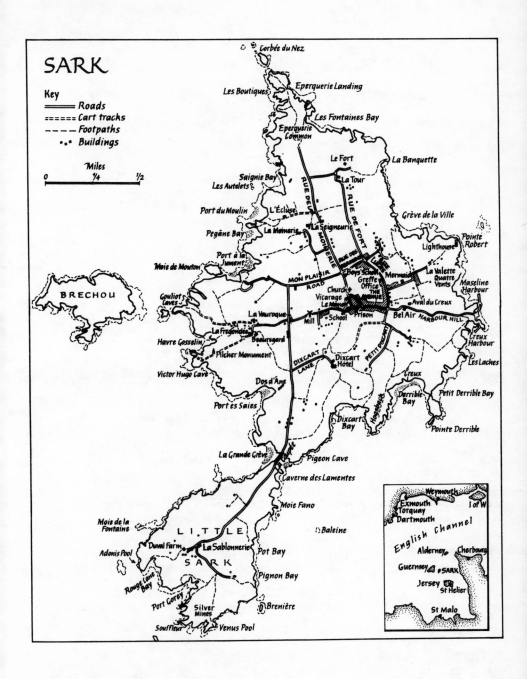

# SARK

**Key**
═══ Roads
═══ Cart tracks
- - - Footpaths
∙∙∙ Buildings

Miles
0      ¼      ½

Corbée du Nez
Les Boutiques
Eperquerie Landing
Les Fontaines Bay
Eperquerie Common
Le Fort
La Banquette
Saignie Bay
La Tour
Les Autelets
Port du Moulin
L'Écluse
Grève de la Ville
Pegâne Bay
La Moinerie
La Seignerie
Pointe Robert
Lighthouse
Moie de Mouton
Port à la Jument
RUE DES
MON PLAISIR
Boys School
Mermaid
La Valette
Quatre Vents
Maseline Harbour
BRECHOU
Gouliot Caves
ROAD
Church
Vicarage
Le Manoir
Greffe Office
THE
Aval du Creux
La Vauroque
Mill
School
Prison
Bel Air
HARBOUR HILL
Havre Gosselin
La Fregondée
Beauregard
Creux Harbour
Pilcher Monument
DIXCART LANE
Dixcart Hotel
PETIT DIXCART
Les Laches
Victor Hugo Cave
Creux
Dos d'Âne
Derrible Bay
Petit Derrible Bay
Port ès Saies
Hogsback
Dixcart Bay
Pointe Derrible
La Grande Grève
Pigeon Cave
Caverne des Lamentes
Moie Fano
Moie de la Fontaine
LITTLE
Baleine
Adonis Pool
Duval Farm
La Sablonnerie
Pot Bay
SARK
Rouge Cane Bay
Pignon Bay
Port Gorey
Silver Mines
Brenière
Souffleur
Venus Pool

Weymouth
Exmouth
Torquay
Dartmouth
I of W
English Channel
Alderney
Cherbourg
Guernsey
SARK
Jersey
St Helier
St Malo

## Out of Call or Cry

*Also by Grace Ingoldby*

**FICTION**

Across the Water
Last Dance With You
Head of the Corner

# OUT OF CALL
# OR CRY

## *The Island of Sark*

### GRACE INGOLDBY

HEINEMANN : LONDON

William Heinemann Ltd
Michelin House, 81 Fulham Road, London sw3 6rb
LONDON    MELBOURNE    AUCKLAND

First published 1990
Copyright © Grace Ingoldby 1990

A CIP catalogue record for this book
is available from the British Library
isbn 0 434 36532 7

Typeset by Deltatype Limited, Ellesmere Port
Printed and bound in Great Britain
by
Mackays of Chatham plc, Chatham, Kent

*To the people of Sark*

In the end all your children move among the scattered acts and memories with no more clues. Not that we ever thought we would be able to fully understand you. Love is often enough, towards your stadium of small things. Whatever brought you solace we would have applauded. Whatever controlled the fear we all share we would have embraced.

MICHAEL ONDAATJE, *Running in the Family*

# Contents

I would like to thank the staff of the BBC Written Archives Centre, the Greffe Office in Guernsey, Sebastian Peake, George Galitzine, Beryl Swain, G. Peter Winnington, Jean Tipping, Richard La Trobe Bateman and Richard Pelerine. I acknowledge my debt to the many writers quoted in the text and particularly to the people of Sark, whose kindness, hospitality and patience taught me so many things not confined to the limits of this book.

# *Prologue*

A place for everything and everything in its place: tide tables hang from a drawing pin stuck into the hot-water tank; binoculars stand ready on the sash. The old man sits at the end of the long kitchen, at the table, by the window, looking out.

A place for everything and everything in its place: shoe horns, tin foil, winter and summer hats. Instructions for the heater, Sark Shipping timetables, a framed coloured print of 'Britons Never Shall Be Slaves' hanging on the wooden wall above the sink. The kettle on the edge of the stove. A picture of mother, always that age now, always that expression, working hands crossed one on the other, placid in her lap.

One worn step down to the scullery; a peg bag in a washing basket, two huge water jars, one zinc, one pottery, covered with a cloth. Liver salts, bubble bath, saddle soap and paint. The gas fridge buzzes an accompaniment to a bikini-waxed Miss UK who twirls on the silent television to an audience of family photographs, an Irish Blessing, a digital wall phone, and a cuckoo clock.

The hatch to the dining room is closed. Heavy furniture, drawers stuffed with knives and forks, egg spoons, tea spoons, yesterdays when the house was booked for the season.

'The cook was from Scotland, her husband used to beat her. She showed me the bruises. One day I caught a conger – like this! She knew how to get the scales out,' the old man makes an inside-out movement with his hand, 'she got the little ones out, at the back. We stuffed it – '

'Herbs?'

'Onions and potatoes. Served it up and they ate it all. A

I

knock came at the door to say, "Same next time"! I moved the TV there but we used to use the serving hatch. She cooked and I washed up, she lay out on a towel and then at eleven I called "Coffee". Every day at eleven o'clock we went fishing. It ran like clockwork.'

It ran like clockwork then. Now, silence in the dining room, hooped-back chairs, souvenir china in a glass cabinet. A signed photograph of Dame Sibyl of Sark on the sideboard, ankles crossed, knitted suit, looks out across white cloths on empty tables, beyond the Gouliot passage towards Brechou. My sister and I, born to snack, eat bread and cheese and cereal, we wash up the little that we use. We are the only guests.

'I met my wife in 1917, an Irish nurse. Always working hard. Working two farms then and building a milking parlour, I wrote "Dairy" in small ormer shells above the door. I built the house in . . . 1923?'

Peeling doors with finger plates, basins wearing skirts. We sleep in tongue-and-grooved wooden rooms that look straight out across the sea. Sleep with the door open, for these old rooms get musty in the heat. Lie on our narrow single beds and read through the long warm afternoons, check how brown we are in an oval railway-carriage mirror on the damp-stained wall.

The old man works rather than potters. He paces himself in days punctuated by television programmes, medicinal whiskies, and – 'Everybody brings me a present' – friends. Up on the roof to mend the water tank, down in one of four sheds looking out that roll of wire – 'I've had this since the Occupation' – waving aside offers of help as he brings the heavy jars of water, hurrying now back to the arm chair covered and tied with blanket, back in time to watch his favourite, *It's Your Dog*.

The days blaze but the nights are cold. It's quiet here, our voices loud in the darkness. We sit out on the stoop in jumpers in the starlight, looking across a wild patch of tall evening primroses. The only sound is the sea coming into Havre Gosselin

2

below us, and in the far distance the orange glow of lights from St Peter Port on Guernsey.

The primroses are for the chop, he says, he'll use the wire to fence this patch, replant it, or perhaps just concrete, a farmer and a fisherman not a bloody gardener. He built the steps down to the harbour, his initials in the concrete there, that was before the war. And he picked up a field telephone, another present from the Germans. That way if he had a good catch he could 'phone his wife from the harbour, say he was going on to Guernsey. 'During the war we ground our corn in the coffee grinder, see the mark left on the table, we didn't mind spending half the night doing it as long as we had something to eat. Everything we ate was natural then, a woman fattening a pig, well that's broccoli leaves for the pig in the evening. . . .' The flu in 1917; the weather as it was: 'You took your jumper off in May and didn't look for it again until October . . . women didn't wear trousers in those days' – we get a sideways look – 'big hats, long dresses. . . .'

Decades drop away as we stand by the kettle, as the television plays on without an audience. Prince Charles visits Brixton, South London, shakes black hands across security barricades. We sit at the kitchen table looking through photographs of grandchildren and great grandchildren. *Murder One* follows the unheeded television news: prosperous Americans, generous mouths full of strong white teeth, hair with body and bounce; a happy family scene intercut by a still of a man in combat gear catching the mother of the family in the sight of a telescopic lens.

Rain in the night, wet and windy, things that were silent creak and groan, sash windows swollen by the damp air grind against their cords and stick. Sea mist that lingers past lunch time, into early afternoon. The old man opens up the little sitting room for us. An upright piano, some prolapsed chairs, a bookcase of holiday reading: *The Cost of a Promise* by Mrs Bealie Reynolds; *Some Eves* by Concordia Merrell; *The Men around Churchill*, Rene Klaus; *Honeypot*, Countess Barckinska.

We are invited in to watch the old man in a television documentary about the island. Everyone knows about it, someone in the family is going to video it – but he does not appear. He is more puzzled and hurt than insulted, and, despite our protestations, convinced that we come from the same world as the television film editors who cut him out of the programme. We know about these things, we come from the world where women wear trousers and don't eat proper meals, we can explain why they cut him out. 'I stood there at the gate and talked to them for over an hour. . . .'

Turn off the lights on the round-pin switches, and the lights at sea go on again. Try and fail to remember what someone, possibly George Eliot, wrote about the lives of ordinary men and women, unmarked graves. Think of the stories holding down this house, the scrape of chairs drawn round the tables in the dining room, fingers that tap the barometer in the porch, secrecy and silence, the bag of grain brought down from its hiding place, crisped in the bottom of the stove, milled in the coffee grinder at the table where now the old man sits alone. The old man, one year older than the century, the oldest man on the island. 'I stood there at the gate and talked to them for over an hour. . . .'

On impulse I fold a piece of paper into a bookmark and stick it between the pages of Mrs Bealie Reynolds, *The Cost of a Promise*. I'm leaving and I can't really tell from his shrewd old face whether he believes me when I say I'm coming back.

# 1

## The Garden of Cymodoce

'Your flight hasn't been called yet if you'd listened.'

Eastleigh airport is a railway station at heart, a branch line with a few dead pigeons in a basket. November is its month.

Autumn 1987, fog, hurricane, fog. I sit eye-to-eye with a single Danish pastry in a clouded cabinet; I sit eye-to-eye with a woman who will not catch my eye. This is a fine start to what is already considered by almost everyone as a typically ill-considered mission, I can't even get to Guernsey let alone the island of Sark.

There are only two boats a week from Guernsey to Sark in the winter. Scheduled flights a week ago were no use to me as bad weather had cancelled the Sark boats. Now the situation reverses with the slow inevitability of heads rolling in a dream. The Sark shipping office is running a boat to the island this afternoon but the flights are fogbound. For me flight delayed means boat missed. I wait until the possibility of a boat recedes entirely, after which I retrieve my baggage and go home.

Fog, hurricane, fog.

Waiting for Wednesday, boat day, to creep around again, I am painting a chair in my daughter's room on an ordinary Sunday morning when news comes in of a bomb at the Cenotaph in Enniskillen, Northern Ireland. News of the death of a child my children played with. In the following days her father's face peers out from the front of every newspaper, the newspapers on the desk from which I phone the airport, eyes drawn down columns of print as the airport keeps me hanging on.

It takes some examination of conscience to mention Enniskillen and Sark in the same breath. Even two years after the event it seems gratuitous, our proximity, but safe – how safe, at several removes – from other people's misery. And yet retrospect reveals that nothing can be written in isolation, events play into our hands and everything belongs to its context. Sark and Enniskillen, this is how it was. This is the world we live in of which Sark is a part; news from Enniskillen reaching Sark via radio, TV, cargo boat.

Here in England – writing in a cold room in what is jokily called the country, in an old house sandwiched between two lethal roads which render birdsong an anachronism; writing with Enniskillen on my desk – even the metaphorical journey to the island is difficult to make. Outside events play havoc with perspective. Perspective has a way of coming to pieces in your hands.

To sit here and read through the written archives on Sark one is struck – it feels like the plop of a marshmallow – by lyricism unleashed, lyricism untamed, wild and free, Sark daubed in with all the artificial colour of a J. Arthur Dixon postcard. A Technicolor vision with a golden hue, sylvan Sark, sweetness and light personified, sepia Sark of sunsets, rainbows, where the sea is blue and the toning prose is purple. Enchanted isle of dells and glades, with its own parliament, its quaint laws, twinkle-eyed fishermen, nut-brown folk. I am reminded of the poet Blake Morrison, who claimed he found twenty words for 'whore' in the Yorkshire dialect when writing his 'Ballad of the Yorkshire Ripper'. The writer on Sark is equally bombarded by linguistic evidence, pastoral with knobs on. All things bright and beautiful, birdsong in the garden on the island the twentieth century forgot.

Forgot or decided not to mention? Sark is very small. It's half a mile longer than the longest runway at London's Heathrow airport, its population could sit comfortably on eleven London buses, would make an average gate for the fourth-division football team Doncaster Rovers. Roughly the same size as Gibraltar, Sark is three miles long and one-and-a-half miles at its widest point; Gibraltar has a population of 30,000, Sark just 550. Who are these people, the islanders, apparently no one knows. This population hardly figures in Sark's archives; when they do appear it's with a walk-on part as folk. Like customers in a shop, one gets the strong impression that they make the place untidy, for books on Sark – and there are lots of them – are in general as neat as they are smug. Once an image of Sark – tiny, outstandingly beautiful, Sark without street lights, without streets, without cars – forms on the retina, everything else is lost. Place is all, people are peripheral. Only one character plays a role in this pile of books and she is Sark herself, Sark, the leading lady, Juliet.

The Dark Ages of Sark are vigorously sketched in by Victor Hugo, exiled to the Channel Islands in the 1850s:

> Formerly, in prehistoric times, the Channel Islands were savage places. The first islanders were probably primitive men of the type found at Moulin-Quignon, and who belonged to the race with sunken jaws. They lived for half of the year on fish and shell-fish, the other half of the year on wrecks. Plundering their coastline was their livelihood. They knew of only two seasons, the fishing season and the season of ship-wrecks, just as the Greenlanders call summer reindeer hunt and winter seal hunt. These islands, later to be Norman, were all thistle-beds, bramble-thickets, and lairs for wild animals and pirates. An old-time local chronicler put it forcefully: Rat-traps and pirate traps.
>
> (VICTOR HUGO, *L'Archipel de la Manche*)

The history of permanent settlement, the consequence of England's increasing maritime trade in the sixteenth century and the French wars which made the Channel Islands ports important, begins with Helier de Carteret, Seigneur of St Ouen in Jersey. As lord at St Ouen he was vulnerable to attack from Sark and recognised the expedience of settling the island which 'might at any time be retaken by the French'. His plan to settle Sark and defend it at his own expense was eagerly accepted by the English.

Helier, the first Seigneur, was granted the Fief of Sark by Queen Elizabeth I in the summer of 1565, his obligation to her, that he would defend it. He apportioned his island into forty strategically sited tenements or holdings. As Helier was obliged to Elizabeth so the tenement-holders, the Quarantine tenants, were obliged to him. In return for a voice and a vote in the island parliament, Chief Pleas, they promised in their turn to take up arms in time of trouble, to give their feudal dues in time of peace.

I have read this passage or variations on it so many times that it now slips effortlessly from pen to page. Most Sark guide books begin with Helier because the way he divided his island and the feudal system he imposed on it can still be seen, like tracks in the grass from the air, on Sark as it is today. Helier is a watershed and watersheds – the First World War, the Industrial Revolution – rule a line through history so neatly and conveniently that they tend to escape our scrutiny, though they are just the sort of monuments that actually block the view. Helier is an obvious choice, a place to start, because what most Sark guide books will go on to tell you is that Sark has hardly changed in essence since 1565. For Sark, like an old actress, is all past. Her attempts to come to terms with the present make the wrong sort of copy. In the darkness of the auditorium one can't make out the faces of its population, all eyes are fixed on Juliet.

Her performance is timeless and bewitching:

Victoria Hotel, Guernsey, May 15th, 1876
Between Saturday morning when I wrote last and
Monday evening when I write now from the same place
but on different paper etc, I have seen on the whole the
loveliest and wonderfullest thing I ever saw – the island of
Sark.
(DAVID SHAYER, *Swinburne the Poet Visits Guernsey and
Sark, 1876*)

Swinburne loved the island, it was just like the Isle of Wight but more so. Its craggy coastline, wreckless sea and furze-covered cliffs provided him with the opportunity to use all his seaside adjectives at once. He didn't take in the people, just the view. In 1855, a contributor to *Household Words*, a periodical edited by Charles Dickens, came and went home equally smitten:

It is, in the first place, very creditable, I think, to any island that it is next to impossible to land upon it – to

8

have no visible harbour, no beach, no sands, no pier, no anything. You may sail round it all day long and perceive nothing but precipitous, barren rocks, which are themselves defended by a cordon of foaming breakers. An inroad upon this bit of British dominion would be a most unprofitable and dangerous business to the most ardent invader, unless he was of a poetical turn of mind. In that case I cannot fancy any spot repaying him so well: if he sailed to the east side and sent out his boats' crews in the direction of a very high seawall, they would perhaps get ashore and be very much astonished at finding themselves then only within a semi-circle of perpendicular rocks; if their noses were turned up, and they followed them further progress would be out of the question; but, supposing them to be otherwise and that they poked them into every crevice and corner, they might hit upon a diminutive tunnel through which, by a very steep hill, they would reach the interior of Sark. I assert that this is the sole method of landing in this island to those who have not been brought up at a gymnasium, or been accustomed to give public entertainments on the tight and slack ropes. A crew of three of us, who arrived here in a little cutter from Guernsey, were deposited on a bare rock at the west end, and directed up an iron ladder which terminated only too soon; leaving us to climb fifty feet of precipice by the aid of a single cord.

A native, who must have seen them coming, carried their portmanteaus to the summit, up, onto and into,

. . . what I still consider after several days' acquaintance, to be Fairyland.

Imagine us at such a height above the sea that the rest of the Channel Islands and France – both a long way off – could be distinctly seen from almost any stand point; the hues of the waves beneath us are wonderfully diversified by sun and shadow; and from the multitude of currents the white breaker crosses the most level blue, and the calmest pool sleeps in the swiftest eddy. Our road, which is at first a narrow pathway, leads by large substantial cottages, as picturesque as those in Westmorland; then by

9

goodly farmhouses, (where it is exchanged for a broad, green cart-lane), with large open court-yards. Both these dwellings are set in garden or shrubbery, and especially decked with untrained, but most luxuriant, fuchsias. We were enchanted and tricked out of our reason. Our luggage seemed to grow lighter on our backs, notwithstanding the noonday sun, and our walk of a mile or so, to good Mrs Hayelhunt's hotel, was a mere May-day procession.

No matter what decade or what century the reader chooses, Juliet continues to pack them in. Though structural engineers have had to shore up the balcony, though even moonlight can't disguise the fact that Juliet now looks a good deal older than her nurse, she still gives a convincing performance:

A poet I know, also Sark bewitched, used to attest that paradise was wrongly named. He died in the sure and certain belief that when about to arise to the celestial region, he would find himself not waiting in hope outside the pearly gates, but filing off the evening boat at Maseline Harbour.
(LEONARD CLARK, *Island of 100 Bays*, BBC Radio, 1956)

The Garden of Cymodoce, so like the Isle of Wight, blooms on across the centuries.

'I thought it looked like old-fashioned England. I think the thing that really strikes you about Sark is, first of all the fact that you arrive by boat, you have to arrive by boat, you cannot fly in and that's rather wonderful. And when you go round it's like being in an Enid Blyton novel. To me it's like England in the fifties, it reminds me so much of the England of my childhood when I used to go to the Isle of Wight. You didn't feel the fields were ever going to be made larger for a start and you felt that no one was going to change it much, that it was all going to go on the same way. Everything's so small and low.'

Sark is small and small is what you make it. Small is beautiful, means almost holy, means the God word community, means sanctions and outcasts, means for the outsider a spurious sense of belonging and the accompanying realisation that there is a longing to belong.

Small means that after just a week on Sark its faces and its places become familiar. Small means that the woman you met at Dixcart Bay – who told you about her disappointing holiday in Skye when, invited to a ceilidhe, she was horrified to be given a slice of Swiss roll rather than a raw herring – seems like an old friend when you meet her again in the Gallery Stores and Post Office. Small means virtually no crime, means parents need not accompany their children to the park – the island is their park and they have the freedom of it. Small means that on the darkest night a woman may walk in a field to look at the stars, or cycle back late in the blackness from a party. Small means the freedom of the city.

Small means gossip and the grapevine, means 'Neighbourhood Watch', means, 'One big eye, One big ear.' Small means if you're talking to the wrong person somebody will catch you at it:

Now Miss Dredger and Miss George had not spoken to each other for over a year. They had ceased to be fond of one another. There had been the question of a right of way across a corner of Miss Dredger's garden. (This short cut would have saved Miss George's legs at least a mile a day, but would have meant that for three hundred and sixty-five days out of the year Miss Dredger would have been liable to see the purple busy in her grounds.) The ugly argument had erupted a year ago and alienated the two of them. So that when Mr Pye suggested that Miss George might like to ride in the carriage while he walked, the effect was horrible. In the stunned silence which followed his ignorant suggestion, Mr Pye turned his head sharply from one to the other. What had he said? Was he already being sucked into the quicksands of island life?
(MERVYN PEAKE, *Mr Pye*)

Books on Sark so dewy-eyed and gooey, so innocuous on first

impression, have a very wilful voice. 'Nothing has changed here or will ever change', Sark in a stoppered glass bottle labelled 'quaint'. Custom's calendar, feudal bliss, enchanted isle – the island the twentieth century forgot hovers in a lyric limbo land between Helier's days and our own. Juliet, like Peter Pan, can never be permitted to grow up.

Sark is small and beautiful and stuck.

> The north limit of this district is the road of Aval le
> Creux, Clos à Jaon onto Beauregard. South limit the
> Coupée, east and west the sea.
> (*Census of Islands in the British Seas*, 1888)

Queen Victoria is on the throne, Sark has its twenty-first Seigneur, but Helier de Carteret the settler, his name lives on. On the night of the census in 1888 there were 312 people living on the island. Carrée, Hamon, Baker, Guille, Mollet, Vibert, Vaudin, le Masurier, le Feuvre, and de Carteret.

> 'Well it's true. Throw up your chin a moment, so that I
> may catch the profile of your face better. Yes, that's the
> d'Urberville nose and chin – a little debased. . . .'
> (THOMAS HARDY, *Tess of the d'Urbervilles*)

Ten surnames predominate. First names are at a premium too. There are three Philip Guilles, three Francis Bakers, two Abraham Bakers.

> The man's calling is usually one of the most common
> means of distinguishing him. In this place where all have
> the same calling this means is not available.
> (J. M. SYNGE, *The Aran Islands*)

Fishermen-farmers, the Sarkese, like the Aran Islanders – men and women who could, through necessity, turn their hand. The average size of a farm is six acres, so Thomas Godfray is doing very well, he owns fifty acres in the Dixcart Valley, flowers in the valley which in the winter has been known to fill with snow.

Philip Guille works five acres in sight of the sea up at Le Fort, Thomas le Masurier has two acres, Joseph Vaudin, now aged forty-seven, has four. Eliza Robin, the schoolmaster's sister, works as a housekeeper at Rue Lucas. Mary Carrée, more in the centre of things, is a general shopkeeper at La Collinette.

Names, ages, occupations and addresses, we open the door and we think we look inside . . .

Peter Hamon is a shoemaker, Lavina Hamon runs the school at La Manoir, Betsy le Feuvre is housekeeper in the north-west of the island near Port du Moulin at l'Ecluse. Two of the Francis Bakers are close neighbours, one a postman, the other a carpenter. They live in the centre of the island on Rue Lucas. Right, past the Bakers to the crossroads of Rue la Rade and Rue du Sermon, in the corner of the square of unmade roads at the heart of the island, another Baker, Elizabeth, a laundress. Elizabeth is forty-six and widowed, head of the family now, five children, but the eldest of them – one a blacksmith, another a labourer – are bringing something in. Her daughter works alongside her in the laundry, the youngest, John and Alfred, are still at school.

1888. Four-fifths of the population were born on the island but anyone over fifty now will remember the heydays of the silver-mining project on Little Sark. The 1830s when the population swelled briefly to 900 and the Coupée which joins Big and Little Sark was loud with the foreign, frowned-on ways of the Cornish tin miners who came – as the oil riggers came to Aberdeen in the 1970s – when expectations were high, and left again when the mines – Le Pot, Vivians, Sarks's Hope and Le Pelleys – failed one after the other.

Joseph Remphrey is the only remnant of those days. In 1842 he married a local girl, Nancy Drillot. Now sixty-one, with four sons, he farms near the highest point of the island, past the mill on the crossroads that leads down to Little Sark, on the corner known as La Vaurocque.

Fishermen, farmers, one ex-miner, ordinary people, everyday life round the base of the monument. Names, ages and addresses, pieces of a jigsaw, facts from which to create a frame. The problem with facts is that facts is all they are, the only thing you can do with them is jiggle them about a bit, create other lists of facts. So at the press of a button the 312 inhabitants sort themselves out under headings. So how many fishermen, how many farmers? Indoor servants, outdoor servants, eight dress-makers, one merchant, two thatchers . . . does any of this get us anywhere at all? The tables are almost narcotically attractive, but still they are only facts. The bones of the skeleton have been slightly animated but still the bones and not the flesh. The facts are hard, are brittle, are dry, the computer tabulates but it is the eye of the beholder that colours the spaces in between.

We dress the characters, in Guernsey sweaters, peaked caps, poke bonnets, pinafores. Indoor servants, outdoor servants, the world where everyone had a station, knew their place?

Four-fifths of the population born on Sark, ten surnames predominate, but biblical warnings on intermarriage don't affect the islanders of Sark. The census column 'Deaf/Blind/Imbecile/ Lunatic' is blank apart from one eighty-eight-year-old, pre-Freud, mad. An untroubled world, the singular world Helier created with its own parliament, its own rules, extended families. Eliza Robin, the schoolmistress, has had some trouble in class with John or Alfred Baker, remember their father is dead. Elizabeth Baker goes down the road to one or the other of the Baker clan to ask for help. . .

Island life at the turn of the century – work hard, play hard, in the face of the wind and the weather. Natural gaiety, honest toil. Photographs of the period now sold as postcards in The Avenue confirm the optical illusion.

The Reverend James Louis Victor Cachemaille and his good dog Trust caught for a moment in the shadow of a porch. A woman in a sun bonnet and a spotless apron draws water from the well near the Rue la Rade at Beau Séjour, hand her a heavy, slopping bucket and she's happy. The track that leads past the tiny cottages at La Fregondée – 'I remember they stood in their doorways there and stared, a hostile place' – is leafy and lush, fishermen mend their pots. A group of girls – favourite occupa-tions helping Mummy, stitching samplers, singing in the choir –

14

straw hats, pinafores, black stockings and boots, pose in a line across the Avenue. The Avenue in the days before the super-market, the bike shop, the gift shop, the Avenue when it was an avenue, shaded by an arch of trees. The windmill grinds the corn and the tithes are given willingly, the Dime Cart makes its horse-drawn journey to the tithe barn at The Seigneurie. . . . Back to the Garden of Cymodoce.

The wells at which those women joyfully collect their water are fern-fringed, wrens jig in thorn bushes, pigs fly. Sark is inhabited by folk who, too mute and humble to utter, offer 'shy smiles' and 'welcoming waves', carry portmanteaus.

Goodly farmsteads, friendly fisher-folk – Patrick Kavanagh's *The Great Hunger* which, to paraphrase the poet Seamus Heaney, shows that the life of a peasant in a secluded spot is not a book of pastoral hours but an enervating round of labour and lethargy, is swept aside at the first sight of the inevitably sparkling, deep blue sea. Francis Baker was the postman, he knew everyone, everyone knew him, 'A true son of Sark', as they say on the gravestones, he belonged. Two thatchers, one watchmaker, Mary Carré at the shop . . . what it represents is deeply attractive.

> On the country has developed the idea of a natural way of
> life, of peace, innocence and simple virtue. . . .
> (RAYMOND WILLIAMS, *The Town and the Country*)

Back at Eastleigh – 'shed-fringed, the airport the twentieth century forgot' – I eventually make it off the tarmac two weeks later than intended, background reading in the forefront of my mind.

Sark so small, 550 people, small enough to hold it, to inspect it, a pebble in the palm? Twentieth-century Sark, Juliet wrestles in mud? Sark where one violent death, that of a child killed on a minefield during the German Occupation of the island in the Second World War, is remembered.

# 2

## Boat Flu

The St. Kildans had little natural resistance to diseases
common on the mainland. They isolated any of their
number who contracted an illness, and were sensibly wary
of visitors who might unwittingly bring disease. A band of
shipwrecked sailors or a party of innocent tourists could
carry common diseases which could be fatal to the
islanders. On Hirta, the people were particularly prone to
catching the 'boat-cold'. So called because it was
invariably contracted after a visit had been paid them by
mainlanders, the boat-cold normally sent every man,
woman, and child on the island to bed.
(TOM STEEL, *The Life and Death of St Kilda*)

The old man is away. The thought that he might not be there to
refer to, to decode messages I bring back, had not even occurred
to me, but he is away and will not be back for weeks at least and
the old house is shut up.

This is my first taste of difficulties to come. Novelists live in a
world of cardigans and cocoa, absorb themselves for months or
years and then expect their family and friends to appear on cue
after the last full stop. The travel writer, equally blinkered, works
from the opposite direction and is surprised and infuriated when
the world she has chosen to describe won't stand still for her but
continues, as it must do, to go round. Everyone she wants to talk
to is either difficult, departed – 'You've just missed him I'm
afraid, what a pity you couldn't have been here last week' – or
very freshly dead.

The old man is away and the BBC tape recorder on which to
capture that idiomatic, faintly South African-sounding speech, is

a mistake. A fine idea on the mainland – 'Remember it must be hand luggage' – it has the effect on the islanders of an unsheathed bayonet.

On a wet and windy Sunday afternoon in November 1987 La Société Sercquiaise meet in The Chalet on Rue de Moulin where the painter and writer Mervyn Peake lived with his family in the 1940s. Arriving members remove their rain hoods and plastic trousers. Galoshes are left in the hall, exchanged for shoes that have bounced their way down in bicycle baskets, like bringing your dancing shoes to a party.

The Société is studious and agreeable, its members meeting once a month to discuss the archaeology, natural history, geology, etc. of the island. It's the sort of gathering in which one becomes conscious of how noisily one eats a digestive biscuit. Nothing else echoes. We sit in chairs and sofas ranged against the walls. Normally gregarious, I'm gagged by the knowledge of what I'm up to, I feel like a burglar caught in the act of casing the joint, I stare hard at what might be the Peakes' old carpet.

> He came back, full of houses that he had seen, one in
> particular, too large, comparatively ugly, but with
> immense space – a daffodil field, a bamboo hedge,
> pampas grass, no light, no electricity, no water, except by
> pumping, but alive, alive, with rooms for possibilities, and
> a whole island to explore.
> (MAEVE GILMORE, *A World Away: A Memoir of Mervyn Peake*)

Years later, when I talk to Peake's eldest son Sebastian, when I tell him about the house there is quiet on the tape I make on my minute and discreet recorder.

'Sark had everything; the wild beaches, the valleys of the Congo, historical allusions to Napoleon with the canons on the cliffs, blown trees. . . .' We talk in a room full of his father's drawings and paintings, the saddest a painting of Sebastian, head in his hand, elbow on the table, the night before he went off to boarding school in Guernsey. Another is of an old Sarkee: 'They used to drink absinthe then. Very rudimentary faces the Sarkese had. I remember one of them got up and tried to hit my father because he'd made the portrait too realistic, they didn't want to be seen like that. Even as a child you were aware of different atmospheres, a sense of cliques; expats.; tea and staff sometimes and muslin over the sandwiches, totally different from eating with the locals.' (Sebastian Peake.)

Fatefully this afternoon is an open meeting, a meeting of the different cliques. Two Sark women have been invited here to talk about the old days and the Occupation. Nothing could be more well intentioned and yet, to an outsider, the meeting is slightly embarrassed, awkward, self-conscious. The 'old days' are the ones before the English had such a toe-hold on the island, though no one mentions this. Juliet is not what she appears to be, the make-up of the population has changed a lot since 1888.

Although sporting a sanitised version of the national costume, the asexual, chest-flattening Guernsey jumper, English residents are easy to spot. Few residents here go native. One senses that a wrist watch ticks beneath the navy rib. Those arms made to lift trestle tables in and out of village halls, those hands that deftly cut the crusts off sandwiches, that tick off points on clipboards, those heads that get together on committees, are terribly familiar. The English abroad these days bring Flymos rather than Bibles, they snip at the grass round staddle stones, they cultivate the bank beyond the hedge and would convert an old washing machine into a window box rather than abandon it out the back. The English are different and, like the weeds this nation of gardeners battle against, invasive. I am not alone. In a sense I am a burglar among burglars.

A nervy benevolence pervades the room on this rainy afternoon. Commitment to the island, contribution to it all through an understanding, empathy with the dispossessed Sarkese, is very much in the air. The English, me included, are well versed on all the available books which cover the Occupation – 'They know it better than you do, they don't know the half of it' – and appear surprised when their stories, the stories from the books, the stories I devoured before I came across, are contradicted, rather than confirmed.

> The visitors who come over to Guernsey nowadays know more about the German Occupation than I do. They have read the books. They know exactly what happened and what didn't, and the whys and the wherefores, and who was going wrong and who was right. I don't. There are those who say, 'Oh, you poor things! It must have been an awful time,' and I say, 'Well, it was, and it wasn't.' There are those who say, 'After all you didn't have such a bad time hob-nob with the Germans,' and I say, 'Well, some did and some didn't.'
> (G. B. EDWARDS, *The Book of Ebenezer Le Page*)

A tale from Dame Sybil Hathaway's autobiography (the Dame was first lady of Sark from 1927 to 1974) is put to the test and found wanting. Her story of how she appeared at the school during the Occupation and picked headlice from the children's hair with an old knitting needle is summarily dismissed, and other anecdotes taken from Julia Tremayne's journal, *War on Sark*, which describes her daily life during those years, go the same way.

'Why did Julia Tremayne say she was stuck in the house because she couldn't go out without shoes, soling her shoes with bar mats, when all of us here used barter when we hadn't got our own?'

Small points, but Sark is small, history isn't dead here, and everything is potentially contentious.

Though everyone is delighted by the afternoon – the old days; school days; days when babies were born on the island; days as one Sark book puts it, 'beneath the German jackboot' – one senses it might have been easier to stick to natural history, the presence on the island of *Crocidura suavolens*, the white-toothed shrew?

Head down, mouth shut, I try not to read the pattern on the carpet that reads 'Juliet's had her day', but it's hard to dispel the suspicion that only when a culture's long dead, brain dead, is it investigated and discussed, embraced in quite this way. I have come in at the tail end of the wake.

Cycling home seems more of an up-hill struggle, the rain seems wetter, grey skies over the Pilcher Monument, low tide, everywhere rocks in the water. It's at times like this that those hours wallowing in literary biographies actually pay off. Lives of the Shelleys and Brontës are obvious pick-me-ups: Shelley on the announcement of the death of another child continues to read *Don Juan*: Charlotte Brontë writes to Mrs Gaskell while the sexton beyond her window digs a grave, and Anne Brontë takes the biscuit by dying standing up. But for the miseries of everyday life Lytton Strachey from any angle is difficult to beat. Lured from his desk with its pneumatic cushion, Strachey really suffered: his trip to see Gerald Brenan in Spain was nightmarish: 'The road was flooded and the journey took twelve hours . . . holding a sunshade over his head and suffering from piles, Lytton repeatedly had to climb on and off his mule on a trip he later described to Virginia Woolf as "death." '

I read Parish Registers, marriages in the late 1830s and early 1840s between the Cornish silver miners and the Sarkee girls.

> July 1839, John Bennet to Mary Anne Guille
> February 1838 Joseph Vincent to Marie Baker
> March 1837 Thomas Rowe to Rachel Hamon

> The laws of the Channel Islands are all more or less feudal but those on Sark are so entirely. The Seigneur has almost every power, save that of life and death, and more than that he has authority. The simple people – who are given in marriage and are forbidden to marry by him, who are expatriated or retained at his pleasure, and to whom the modern comforts and elegances of his residence appear to be the possessions of a superior being – do absolutely pay homage and obedience willingly and without cavil.
>
> (*Household Words*, 1855)

'When we were boys and we saw the Seigneur come along we used to form a guard of honour and we would say, "Good morning Seigneur," and he would say, "Morning boys," and if we didn't we wouldn't have a break for a week. I once told the Dame that.'

'People used to respect age, the older generation, but I don't think they do that now, Christian names are used more, I still can't manage that. Sark had the same school teacher for fifty, sixty years and he taught us respect. If we hadn't respected the Seigneur . . . well . . . he was very strict. We used to go round to the Seigneurie to count the tithes, never the front door.'

'When they make a film they always make it seem – it's just a load of people whizzing round on carriages and tractors and bikes. They talk about the history, the Seigneur, it's the Dame mainly they go on about. The Dame made herself known. You can just pass the Seigneur and think he's a normal person. I don't think him any different. I know he does something but I don't see what, no evidence of what he does.'

The Seigneur deals with journalists and writers. It is November and the main gates which let tourists into the Seigneurie gardens in the summer are shut. I cycle through the farm and end up bang in front of the large and suitable seigneurial house, a huge fallen tree felled by the hurricane – conversation point – lies across the grass. In the atmosphere of cultural drift which seems to personify Sark in the late 1980s it is hard to work out where to prop the bike.

We talk in a small drawing room. The Seigneur, Michael Beaumont, inherited Sark when his grandmother, La Dame, who 'made herself known', died in 1974. He talks quietly and politely but obviously finds it difficult to muster any excitement for yet another project based on Sark. Enter Boat Flu.

'I see at least one journalist a week, I'm sure you'll understand

21

that I don't allow access to any archive material. We get a little tired seeing the same old phrases churned out yet again.'

'What sort of phrases?'

'The island with no divorce. The island that allows you to beat your wife, that sort of thing, anything that's quaint.'

He fields questions on the not-so-quaint Guernsey tax laws which have brought money to individuals on the island who work as off-shore directors, assuring me that the 'trickle-down theory' works on Sark, the new rich are generous to the island which has made them rich, they behave like Robin Hood.

The island exchequer turns on £150,000 a year, they can only afford to pay the doctor £6,000, and have to try and find someone who not only fits in but can afford – just before retirement perhaps – to take this cut in pay. He'd like more for education, for the old. Talk turns stickily once more to the benefits, 'the contribution made' by the off-shore directors, known here as 'The Sark Lark', then moves on to safer ground of the equivalent of *Crocidura suavolens*, classical concerts held in the Seigneurie gardens in the summer.

We talk for over an hour, although nothing much seems to be said, and end as we began on the subject of 'people like me', the journalists, the perennial questions, the old chestnuts. 'So how do you see the future, Mr Beaumont?'

The article archive remains in his care. The fact that it exists at all, that the making of it, those interviews with other journalists, induced boredom and irritation in equal measure, is more enlightening than what it may contain.

Films and radio programmes on Sark are the opposite of the 'get-your-arm-around-a-gorilla' school. They begin at Creux, the old harbour, more photogenic than La Maseline. Creux bustles with folk one or two of whom – well I never – still speak the old Norman-French patois: 'The islanders are all characters, the closeness to the sea and the seasons seems to produce strong characters. So' – close-up of character – 'What happened here during the Occupation? So' – close-up of lobster pot – 'this is a real old-fashioned lobster pot?'

Up the harbour hill – screech of gulls, clop of carriage horses –
and hot-foot to the Seigneurie. A shot of the dovecot – 'The
Colombier is the exclusive right of the island's Seigneur' – the
apple mill, the Dime Cart, ah, there he is standing by the cannon,
'How do you see the future, Mr Beaumont?'

Down to the school which doubles as the island parliament,
Chief Pleas. 'Here the children may leave at 15.' Time now to
swop a few platitudes – 'No party politics here' – with the
Seneschal, the island magistrate: 'So how does it feel to be
Seneschal?' A minute or so with the Greffier, the clerk, to find out
how he's feeling, and, in radio documentaries, sound-effect
delirium: gulls, hammers, neighing horses, swearing in Sark
patois, trill of bicycle bells, boom of cannon, clash of lobster pots,
the blacksmith at his anvil.

The blacksmith, once an ordinary man, is now rather rattled
by cameras, microphones and notebooks. 'What do you think I
am?' he asked me, stepping out of character, when I braved the
forge for a performance. 'A parrot on a stick?'

> In the lion house they walked slowly from cage to cage
> until they came to a tiger which walked up and down, up
> and down, up and down, turning his great painted head
> with intolerable familiarity, and with his whiskers just
> brushing the brick wall. . . . 'They pay for their beauty
> poor beasts . . . mankind want to catch anything beautiful
> and shut it up, and then come in their thousands to watch
> it die by inches.'
>
> (DAVID GARNETT, *Man in the Zoo*)

Although both television and radio narrators never fail to remark
upon what they see as the positively somnambulant pace of Sark,
the documentaries have a breathless feel. Out of the forge and on
to the Elizabethan cannon, the German anti-tank gun (not much
use during the Occupation and abandoned after it), across La
Coupée, the bridge that joins Big and Little Sark, a shot here of
the old silver mines perhaps, then back to the harbour and with
sad farewells – welcoming waves run backwards? – home.

23

'They're used to the media, aren't they? The articles are always the same. There were some Americans filming in the Seigneurie gardens, Sark feudal system again. It's so positive all the time, it would be nice to see what it's really like, not the magic of Sark, that sort of thing. The Occupation, that's all been done. People are so much the same, is anyone more interesting here than anywhere else? The old business of the characters again, the characters of the island, portrayed like fairings.'

> Educated people in England, if they consort with members of the working classes, tend to think of them as 'characters'. You may throw darts with the yokels in the village pub but all the time the yokels are on the stage and you are in the stalls. Instead of a bouquet for their performance you give them a pint of bitter.
> (LOUIS MACNEICE, *The Strings are False*)

'Harry Secombe came. He said, "I want you to come to the Eperquerie next morning, I'll sing you a song. I've made a song for you." And he sang it, "Always a friend", he just made it in one night, no music, stood there and sang that song. I mean the way he done it, I could have wept, such a genius man. And now he's made it up I could sing it for generations, "Always a friend", ah, it was beautiful, two years ago he came, in the September.'

'I never got on the book because I kept hiding behind all the doors. The photographer, he liked an old-fashioned farm and he took . . . I don't know how many pictures . . . and he was here every day and yet people come in here who don't understand about farming and they say, "Oh God, it's awful." '

The BBC Written Archive Centre has a little file on Sark. Researchers sit in a small room in a converted bungalow in Reading. The deputy editor of the *Observer* shares my desk and keeps the pencil sharpener firmly on his side. I think that rubbing shoulders with him in the canteen might further my career but am whisked off at lunchtime to a pub in the country by a writer of

Chinese horoscopes. Back at the desk the voice that emerges through the files of a 1938 documentary, *Welcome to Sark* by Francis Dillon, sounds familiar:

> 'Brandy, 3d a glass. What's the hurry? 3d a glass, I'm
> going to live 'ere.'
>     'Look at the old boy with the whiskers, doesn't he look
> a character!'

A letter in this file, from the Dame to the Producer, says that she will be pleased to help with the documentary, wouldn't consider asking payment for herself, but suggests that the islanders ought to be paid. The word she uses for islanders is peasants, the word leaps off the page, it's like reading a letter from Tolstoy. The *Oxford Dictionary* provides a definition of 'peasant' from 1613: 'Serf, villein; also boor, clown.' This is, or was in 1938, the world the twentieth century forgot. Peasant in Sark, like peasant in China, was a noun without pejorative meaning. If there is a lord of Sark, a seigneur, then it follows that there must be peasants, and the Dame, who called a spade a spade, got what she asked for. Contributors to the documentary were paid five or six shillings each and a guinea for 'notables'.

The present Seigneur deals with journalists. Quaint laws, women in bonnets patting butter, and particularly lobster pots are part of his grandmother's legacy:

> The journalists appeared to find her an ideal subject,
> intelligent, alert and with an instinctive knowledge of the
> kind of information they most needed for their articles on
> the 'woman feudal ruler of a tiny kingdom' – as many
> termed her.
>     (BARBARA STONEY, *Sibyl, Dame of Sark*)

In the 1930s she travelled to America on the *Queen Mary* to give a series of talks illustrated by slides. The Americans loved her – there is nothing like a Dame:

> The impression that Sibyl often gave on this tour, that
> Sark was rather more feudal and its people more
> subservient than they in fact were, annoyed some of the
> islanders. . . . But she had long ago discovered that such
> exaggeration of her position not only increased the interest
> in herself but in Sark as a whole – particularly in those
> countries without monarchies of their own.
> (BARBARA STONEY, *Sibyl, Dame of Sark*)

'I was so incensed by that biography that I read it to the end. She
had never met her even. I destroyed it. I was furious about it, I
wouldn't let anybody have it, I destroyed it. I wouldn't keep it in
the house because it wasn't true about things she only knew
through hearsay. She had not met her. To publish a book like
that. . . . La Dame didn't hide her faults, her wildness when she
was young, did she? The autobiography was wonderful.'

'Just imagine what would happen if the Seigneur was a real
villain. If Sibyl Hathaway had done more wicked things than she
did do maybe the whole system would have had to be terminated.
Her lecture tours didn't do it, it's part of the twentieth-century
disease, if she didn't do it someone else would have done.'

> At the beginning of every lecture . . . I used to try to
> convey the atmosphere of the island by saying that the life
> we lead is entirely different from that in America. No
> motor-cars, no income tax or death duties or surtax, no
> unemployment, no trade unions, no politicians. . . . Sark
> is not, however, a sort of feudal pageant to amuse visitors.
> It is a real live community of people who are happy to
> have retained their ancient form of government, and
> possess a subtle dignity of their own, born of many years
> of independence, honourable work and satisfied old
> age. . . . I had undertaken the lecture tour in the hope
> that it would bring American visitors to us. . . . I
> constantly find that I am greeted by tourists who stop me
> to say that they met me after one of the lectures.
> (DAME OF SARK, *Autobiography*)

'Half the people know about the Dame of Sark, half of them think she's still alive don't they?'

Conscious of Sark's heritage, its version of the boat-cold, frightened of the blacksmith, I cycle the island in the rain. I love the island, with a 'coming home' love that's totally unfounded and difficult to explain. I love it even, perhaps especially, in this empty month out in the squalls of wind and rain. Hardly another bike passes, doors and windows shut against the weather, the sea round every corner, boiling grey. I love it but I feel it turn against me as I prod and poke at Juliet. Ambassadors on every corner, official-speak born of boat flu. Hans and Lottie had it easy, falling backwards off the stern of boats, filming shoals of fish.

'You get very irritated when you've spent a great deal of time trying to explain to somebody exactly how Sark works and when you read their article you learn they miss the point completely. And, after it happens five or six times you think, what's the point in talking to people. They have come here with an idea, they are looking for points in what I'm saying to illustrate that idea and to hell with what it's actually like. You can't help putting everything through your mind and your mind is going to put your interpretation on it. I've decided, this is my point of view and if they don't want it they can lump it, but some people will produce with infinite patience what they want to hear.'

> The greater number of those who have written about
> Sark have made strange mistakes in the matter and have
> represented the Seigneur in a somewhat singular and
> sensational light. Few of those who have taken upon
> themselves to describe Sark have made a sufficiently
> lengthened stay to enable them to gather correct
> information; they have sought rather to amuse their
> readers with absurd exaggerations.
> (LAURA E. HALE, introduction to *The Island of Sark*, 1928)

'She went off her nut over that book didn't she, really and truly, oh yes. She . . . I remember . . . well I don't remember her going off like that, but I used to work for the old Seigneur, the Dame's father, and the two Miss Hales, Pattie and Laura, were great friends of the old man and they used to come one afternoon a week and have tea with him and all the rest – and she was writing that book then – she went dotty.'

Journalists are never alone on Sark and, depending how long they've been there and how miserable they are, they meet like conspirators in the darkest corners of cafés, to whisper, giggle and sob.

'There's an American on the island doing what you're doing. He has a long beard.'

'Anthropologist, he's been here ages. I used to see him around, think what a strange-looking chap he was but I never really heard. . . .'

'He's been here three months already. A beard? I'm not sure, but he lives near Le Fort.'

'He camps in a field near the Mermaid Tavern. . . .'

'He's living near the lighthouse, down by Point Robert.'

I have a small baby, he has a small beard, we finally meet by accident when he spots the 'baby carriage' outside the Dan San Café in the Avenue. He has his science, anthropology, to hide behind, but he doesn't seem much braver than I am, here is a man who's known low tide.

An anecdote about the anthropologist goes like this: At the beginning of his project the anthropologist went into the Greffier's office and asked what had happened on Sark during this century. Towards the end he went back and said, 'I understand you now. Nothing.'

The anthropologist has been on Sark three months and is nearing the end of his stint. He talks about the importance of making firm appointments with interviewees: 'Pin them down to Wednesday at 2.00.' His method is to make a contentious statement and then tick the appropriate box: 'agree, disagree, disagree strongly, dispute, etc.' This bald approach leads on, if it works, to explanation and justification; statistics, tables, crude marriage graphs, circular diagrams and breakdowns emerge. Unfortunately he hasn't a single graph on him when we meet and does not reply later when I write, but he does give an interview to the *Guernsey Evening Press* before he leaves:

> There is a theory held by leading anthropologist Eric Woolf which says that: 'The expansion of the economy throughout the world affects everybody not just directly but indirectly, and you can see the effects of capitalistic expansion in many local populations. . . .' Sark is like other isolated societies in other parts of the world in that it is being affected by the outside world. The results will be compared with many other studies of this nature. He was rather surprised, however, that the majority of people do not seem to worry about the future and particularly not this aspect of it. He said that Americans, in similar circumstances, would be a lot more concerned, but 'time and time again I was told it is a Sark saying, "We will see what happens." '

The anthropologist is keen on watersheds and puts his up after the Occupation. Captain Ernest Platt, author of *Sark as I found it* (1927), put his up after the First World War:

> A gallant officer. . . . He has seen much of life up and down the world but possibly the greatest victory will be set down by psychologists as won when he went to Sark, saw it, and remained there to be acknowledged one with the Sarkees, the most limited, and jealousy conserved autonomy in the world.

Both of us seem likely to be set down by psychologists on a couch. The fact that when we meet, though we could hardly be more conspicuous, we are both wearing broad red and white stripes is the extent of our bravado. We begin by talking business and quickly descend to idle gossip and speculation, the stuff of island life.

Later in the pub – what a relief for both of us, to be a two, a crowd – we agree, 'strongly', that suspicion and resentment, and over-exposure – boat flu – make life on Sark hard going. The anthropologist explains, though I already understand, that he has to poke his nose in, it's part of his job, but on bad days can scarcely poke his nose out of his tent. Despite the lack of graphs which might have come in handy, I seem to be cast in the role of his consoler. I have just re-read *The Aran Islands* and am struck by how much time Synge spent lying down. Told by Yeats to forsake the boulevards and go to the edge of Ireland 'to express a life that has never found expression', he was often prone:

> As I lie here, hour after hour, I seem to enter into the wild pastimes of the cliff and to become a companion of the cormorants and crows.

Synge was also subject to the departed/freshly dead rule and there is never any news:

> I returned to the middle island this morning. . . . Old Pat Dirane is dead, and several of my friends have gone to America; that is all the news they have to give me after an absence of many months.

The plight of Robert Flaherty, the American documentary film-maker, puts Sark boat flu into perspective. We giggle hysterically over it, it really cheers us up.

In 1931 Flaherty was travelling to England and got into conversation with a young Irishman on the boat who told him of a 'place off the West Coast of Ireland . . . where the struggle for bare subsistence made booms and slumps look silly.' Giving up the idea of shooting 'Man against the Sea' in Samoa Flaherty headed west:

> 'Every other person in the Aran Islands,' Flaherty said, 'has the name Flaherty or O'Flaherty. . . . There were some who were quite sure we had assumed the name in order to gain their confidence.' Flaherty was not a Roman Catholic . . . and wild rumours about him circulated

among the islanders. He carried a bottle of water, the rumour went, with which he would sprinkle children and turn them into protestants. And since the unit landed a flower had started to grow, which if it spread would lead the people to damnation.

(ARTHUR CALDER MARSHALL, *The Innocent Eye*)

# 3

# *Land of Our Fathers*

'When I first went there I still saw men walking the field with a leather pouch sowing their seed. Quite a bit was still being cut with a sickle and they were content to do it, they knew no other way.'

'None of the peasants would have wanted to continue in agriculture anyway. The peasant economy is bloody hard work, it's absolutely killing and back-breaking. The one thing that has changed people's lives above everything else is electricity, not the motor car. The motor car has increased their convenience and disrupted their life but electricity has taken the drudgery, the killing, back-breaking drudgery out of so many things. It's still hard work running a farm but by comparison to what it was. . . . Electricity came to Sark just after the war and that brought with it the real change in people's expectations.'

Of all the people I met on the island it was the Sarkee farmers and their wives who, once the ground between us was established, were eager to talk, were hard to stop once we got going. The farmers – who lit me across the thresholds of old sheds in the winter, who invited me into their houses, gave me drinks and cakes and cigarettes – made me feel a friend.

Where once almost everyone was a farmer-fishermen, there are now half a dozen farms. A Young Farmers club on Sark would be lucky to get three members. Most are in their late seventies. It is their age and the changes they have seen that kept us talking in dark byres and soaking fields, in parlours with the TV turned down low, across kitchen tables at the end of another hard day.

The plus side of farming on Sark, the lack of interference, the absence of bureaucracy, can be read between the lines of our conversations; it is not mentioned specifically because independence is taken for granted here, independence is not considered a privilege but a right. The old chestnuts that farmers live like lords off what's inevitably called 'the fat of the land', that farmers are always complaining, has some truth in it, but thinking back on those conversations that often went on long into the night, the image of a bewildered and beleaguered group remains with me, of men and women genuinely isolated and worn down.

Traditionally vraic, seaweed, was cut in the bays and carted to the farms where it was spread on the land as fertiliser.

'Seaweed fertiliser? Ever since I remember there hasn't been a lot used. I did try it and it's very good, of course now you don't know if it's contaminated. We used to winch it up from the bay down there, in my father's time we used to use a horse and then we got an engine. I've done it with a tractor. I bought a tractor, an International, in 1910 and I was still using it after the war. Diesel, one year I ran it on petrol, it lasted twenty-five years with a reconditioned engine. I pulled vraic with a tractor but you wouldn't get anybody these days to do that sort of work. We haven't got the seaweed now, there's about half the seaweed down in the bay as there used to be, perhaps it's because it's not been cut? We used to cut it in the bay, down in Greve de la Ville, used to be tons of it. Years ago we used to clear the bay nearly every year.'

'I can remember the good times at the Grand Plough. Early in the morning each tenant brings his horse or horses to one farm. That farm is ploughed and the next day they move to another farm until all the holdings are ploughed. It isn't just a job, it's a festival, a carnival of ploughing. There's always plenty of whatever the men prefer to drink, gin, brandy, beer or cider, and many hands made not only light work but high spirits and gaiety. Then in the evening when work is done, everyone gathers at the

33

farm where the land has been ploughed that day to eat, drink, dance, sing and play old games.' (SIBYL HATHAWAY, Francis Dillon BBC Radio documentary, 1938)

'Things have changed completely since the war and we've got too many English residents, that's the trouble. Well it's the Sark people's fault, they shouldn't have sold their property but, then again, fabulous prices were offered. I know very well my son will sell my place if he ever gets it. When the farmers die Sark will just be a resort for millionaires.

'Most of the young people now they don't want to bother with cattle and that sort of thing, there's much easier money on the carriages. They don't want any responsibility, they don't want to work, that's what it amounts to. This is a place that, I think – I know I'm a bit old-fashioned now – but I think there's quite a lot of jobs that have got to be done by hand to do well, and today, if anything can't be done by machine, it's not going to be done. The young chaps of today, they wouldn't do what we did when we were young, they haven't got the stamina, I don't think they could even if they wanted to.

'We used to be all day ploughing, deep ploughing with six or eight horses, that was really, really a day. Start about eight in the morning till nearly dark in February, March, do the chores with the animals, dance half the night and then next morning, out on the ploughed ground harrowing with the horses again. I think the food has got a lot to do with it, why the young are so soft nowadays. I mean in those days we had stuff quite different to what they're eating today, we made our own bread right up to the war.'

'I hated farming. I hated the fact that the animals had to be slaughtered. It was day in, day out, with no future.'

'I think it's tragic, it's sad that the Sarkese have allowed farming to decline, but you see they earn so much more money than they could ever earn with farming and in this day and age money counts. When I lived there the people weren't nearly so emancipated as they are now, no TV, nothing at all. There wasn't such a thing as a bore hole on the island, everyone went to a well. I drew every drop of my water, let a bucket down and drew it up myself, no other means at all. There has inevitably been a change of attitude to life with the Sark people, particularly the younger ones, it's inevitable. They have grown up to a different way of life, definitely, since the 1950s, they have come into the twentieth century. They had never seen a train and I don't know if they'd ever been over to Guernsey, you see. Their life was Sark, their world was Sark and they were in a way far more content because they knew nothing else.'

They prod us with cameras, making us aware of what we
    do.
                            (ALISDAIR MACLEAN, *At the Peats*)

Sark cows, Jerseys, are tethered in the fields which are hedged and mostly unfenced, and are milked there either by hand or portable machine. I sit on the headland and talk to a farmer who cannot sell his milk or butter, sit in the drizzle as he milks endlessly into a bucket, one cow taking over forty minutes. The farmer is in his late seventies, he has stopped feeding concentrates to his herd of four because he says that concentrates consist of the 'bits and pieces' of other animals, particularly sheep. He blames concentrates for driving one old milker mad. Our conversation is topical and informed enough to fill the leader column in any serious newspaper. The farmer, unaware of the labels 'green' or 'organic', has arrived at his point of view from a mixture of experience and philosophy and is quite unconscious of the weight now being given to what he says. What he considers to be straightforward and old-fashioned has become, ever more so in the two years of the writing of this book, to be thought of as enlightened and environmentally sane. As if to confirm this anomaly a tourist, walking politely around the edge of the field, quite obviously euphoric at the sight of an old character milking a beast by hand, moves gingerly towards us and takes our photograph as we sit there in the rain; only the cow looks up.

35

'At the moment I'm worried how long we are going to be able to continue, how long we can earn a decent living on the farms. At one time milk and beer were the same price, now no one wants milk, butter, cream or meat. So what have you got? I can't get an answer. I'm a bit worried because I've got three cows I've got to slaughter, how am I going to get rid of the meat? Okay I've got deep freezes, I can possibly put one in, I can't put three. I think I may be able to get rid of them but it's going to be with a struggle. Not only the hotels won't take local meat, a lot of them won't take local cream or local milk. You've only got to be down at the harbour when the cargo boat comes in to see the amount of cream that comes over and sometimes milk. You see, what's going to happen? The EEC have only got to say, okay, get French milk over. Up to now they've put a bit of a stop on it. The French milk is supposed to last for what . . . about five weeks? Don't tell me it's like the milk you're getting here. I mean, the milk you're getting here is as good as the cream you're buying in Europe without bragging at all.

'It's always been the same. At this time of the year, August, we're more or less always a bit on the short side, we try to get our animals organised so that they calve in the spring. Now I've got one cow and one heifer, it'll calve at the end of September, I'll have to turn that into butter, we can't use it. We have a fellow in Guernsey that buys cream off us, but again, I rang him up the other day if he wanted a bit more and he said no and he said what they're asking for is butter. If anybody knew the amount of work there is to make butter in the summer, and by the time it's made it's so soft you've got to cool it down somehow or other before you can work it. One and a quarter pints of cream makes one pound of butter, there's no profit in it whatsoever. And another thing people don't realise is that our job is 365 days a year.'

When Sybil Hathaway, later La Dame, took over Sark in 1947 she caused some controversy by putting up a notice in the village offering half a crown a day for children who would count the tithes:

She had decided after all to reimpose the dixieme, the levy of one-tenth of all cereals grown on the island which they had allowed to lapse since the early years of the war. When some of the farmers protested at its reintroduction, the international press were quick to seize upon the opportunity it gave to attack Sark's feudal system. The *News Chronicle* of 23rd September reported one Sarkese as saying: 'We consider ourselves held in bondage in perpetuity. Farmers inherited their farms with their obligations. To refuse would in effect mean disinheritance and to be forced off the island. We in Sark know that Feudal bondage in an age of advancing democracy is a mockery of modern civilisation. . . .'

(BARBARA STONEY, *Sibyl, Dame of Sark*)

The Dame retaliated by saying that there was no hardship in the tithes and that the trouble was that the islanders had grown too prosperous, that an increase in visitors to the island had made them 'lazy and slack. . .'.

'At one time practically every farm was worked by the owner, now you can name the farmers on one hand, about ten. But what sort of farmer? A farmer is a man who works his land, gets what he can out of it for his animals. I mean years ago there was a lot of parsnips grown, a lot of corn grown, now it's chiefly down to grass. Years and years ago they had the land in rotation. First of all in turf they grow parsnips, after the parsnips were dug up they put wheat, after the wheat it was ploughed up again the following year, they'd put oats and undersow it to grass and that was the rotation. Occasionally they put a patch of mangels or swedes in between. In those days there were no concentrates, about fifty years ago. When I was a school kid, my grandfather . . . anybody at that time, anybody growing corn . . . it was all bundled and when it was ready to be carted the children would be paid on their holidays to go wherever they were sent to count the bundles. When you finished you'd take your paper to say how many bundles there were so the Seigneur could send the Dime Cart to collect the tithes. At that time at the Seigneurie there were four or

37

five really big stacks of corn and most of it had come from tithes. Every tenth bundle and in our language, ten means "di". The barn is still there at the Seigneurie, next to where they put the wood, it was all given up at the end of the Occupation.'

'There were wooden scales for the corn, they had a small measure which was called a cabot, there are still tithes that go to the Seigneur at different times, paid in money. The Seigneur – I owe him six cabots. Some of it has dwindled away, for instance, the field at the Clos des Camps is built on. It used to belong to X's mother and she owed thirty cabots for that field every year and she asked Dame Sibyl to buy it outright instead. The place I owe six cabots for? At one time there were thirty on that property. Dame Sibyl's grandfather wanted to make a path from the Seigneurie over Saigne Bay to get to the Eperquerie and just on my field there was a little spot that was no good for anybody – up to the hedge – so rent was reduced in cabots for that bit.'

> Retraite: The legal right of the near relatives of a vendor of a property to buy back the property by paying the purchase price to the buyer within a stated period, which varies according to circumstances. In the case of inherited property, only kinsfolk of the male line of the vendor can exercise this right, but if this property was originally purchased by the vendor, and was not inherited, kinsfolk of both the male and female lines of the vendor possess the right to exercise retraite.
>
> (*Fief of Sark*)

'I retraited the tenement, Petit-Beauregard. X's father, when I started at Beauregard, he said, "At last a farm is in Petit-Beauregard." There was a pathway and you had to walk single-file, brambles, gorse, the hedge went thirteen feet into the field. He'd left it you see, right through the Occupation. He was a fisherman, he just grew potatoes and I think he kept a cow or two but not really to earn a living out of it.

'Now the people I let the house to are just like one of us. They give a helping hand if necessary and when we're digging the potatoes they help pick them and that and they never want any payments so you can give them potatoes for the winter and what have you.

'If you want anything then work for it then, if you've got the money buy it. There were a lot of farms at that time that could have been retraited but weren't and once they got into English possession, I mean – it's hard to get it back. One or two of them have been got back lately but with the price they have been sold it is a bit awkward, hundreds of thousands of pounds for farming land.'

In press interviews Sibyl was quoted as saying that agriculture had deteriorated to 'a shocking state' owing to the occupation of farmhouses by English residents who 'neglected the cultivation of formerly tilled land, some of which had been allowed to run to waste.'
(BARBARA STONEY, *Sibyl, Dame of Sark*)

'It's more difficult to retraite now because everything's gone sky high. When I was working for anybody as a young man, my biggest wages were 25 shillings a week. My father didn't think I was mad to do it because he was a businessman. Several times he was on the verge of selling the farm. We are well provided for now because I can pay my way even if they have to sell some of the animals to bury me.'

At harvest time the reapers cut the corn with sickles as their ancestors did 400 years ago in the same fields.
(LEONARD CLARK, *Island of 100 Bays*)

'When we started off the corn had to be cut by hand, just mowers, all bundled and restacked. The combine is the best invention of the twentieth century, you just put it in and by the time it's finished you've got it thrashed and winnowed and ready to use.'

'If you're prepared to stick to the same line in farming all the time and let the world pass by . . . it's like the hare and the tortoise –

39

the farmer may be a tortoise but he'll definitely get there. There are two or three things in farming, if you wanted to grow your vegetables and your animals it could be an occupation for quite a few. I think there's a big future in farming, not to make a fortune but to live. That about all you do is live.'

> From the moment a roof is taken in hand there is a whirl of laughter and talk till it is ended, and, as the man whose house is being covered is a host instead of an employer, he lays himself out to please the men who work with him.
> (J. M. SYNGE, *The Aran Islands*)

'I remember in 1938 we were in the same position as we are now, because you can't get anybody to work on the land now, people won't work those hours. In 1939 we had three hundred bundles of bracken on the common which had to be brought up on our backs. We had five or six people helping us one afternoon and we finished. Now I said, "What do we owe you?" and they said, "Forget about it. You give us a few potatoes, few parsnips or carrots. . . ." That sort of thing happened all through the Occupation. The fact is – all these strikes – there's one going now in Guernsey about the postmen. I mean postmen don't work hours like we do and it's for money again. Practically all the strikes are for money at the end, the more they get the more dissatisfied they get and the more they want, it's a vicious circle.'

'They had to farm their land or they wouldn't have had a living. The tourists that came in those days, they didn't add enough, they had to farm their land, they kept themselves going and they grew their own vegetables. They had their own meat on the island. They now have far more prosperity, far better homes, more money and that is wonderful for them but I think though they have gained enormously they have lost something too, definitely.'

'It's easier for people to buy freezer meat from Guernsey isn't it, already sorted out, minced and boned. Fish? People want fish fingers. I can't shift the meat I slaughter. We used to salt down beef and fish but the last lot of fish we did the salt was not the same as the old coarse salt. Nothing's as good. In the old days using the gorse in the big ovens, to smoke fish and ham, hang it up in a muslin sack in the chimney. Pet pigs were kept in the house for six weeks, they house-train easily, vicious when they're put out though and the first opportunity they're back to the Rayburn. They miss the house and they never forget it, one pig she never forgot as soon as your back was turned she made a bee line for the house and lay down by the Rayburn.'

'We worked together, the wife and I, and if cross words were spoken she would come out or I would go in from the fields and apologise, "I'm sorry", kiss and make up.'

'Farming is a family business, yes. When I got married in 1936 I had nothing. I had £36.00 in the bank when I got married and that went to pay for the wedding, don't forget it cost me 7 shillings and 6 pence to buy the wife!'

'There could be market gardening if somebody wanted to put some work into it, easily, because it's cheaper to buy local than it is from Guernsey but some say they would rather import because that is a sort of guarantee. If there were tomatoes on the island then one would stop buying Guernsey. We don't grow tomatoes because we couldn't fly them out, and they might spoil by boat. Tomatoes for locals are a possibility, I think it's lack of interest on the island.

'We pick our own potatoes and there are patches of parsnips and carrots which used to be grown but unfortunately are not grown that way any more. We never used to import, right up to the 1950s we never imported vegetables, there was no need because we all grew and gave to one another. Importing vegetables is a sacrilege to my way of thinking. Lack of labour stopped the vegetables. The hammer came along, all this building, big wages. It changed overnight, just like that. As soon as the big wages came the farmer couldn't afford those big wages

41

so they had to change their way of farming. In one way the island became too prosperous in the wrong direction. Farming is seven days a week, you've got to be dedicated to farming for life.'

'We used to run home from school, my grandfather was working the farm at that time and the first one back could milk the easiest cow.'

'We have our own slaughterman on the island and we have to be our own vets a lot of the time. I'm the only one of the island with a flutter valve for milk fever. A vet would inject a cow into the blood stream but I do it in between the skin and I show the younger men. I'm a great believer in showing the young ones what you know. Once you've gone. . . . The wife had an uncle who showed me quite a lot, also my father doing his own veterinary work. I remember an evening on Little Sark; there was a cow with milk fever, it was snowing like mad, we couldn't take the tractor across La Coupée, another tractor met us at the other side. Coming back it was horrible, we could hardly stand but we managed it and saved the animal whereas if it had been left to the morning she'd have been gone.

'I've won cups for my cattle at the cattle show here. We judge the cows with a bag full, you've got to milk them on the field and then they judge them after. I've won the Queen's Cup for best cow on the field.'

'The pattern of farming has changed, with the horses on it all year round a lot of the land's no longer any good.'

'We are a family and we're lucky, if you haven't a family you can understand them selling their farms, there's no point. Why struggle with a farm if you've got no one following who's interested?

'We farmers are not as spoon-fed as they are on the mainland, we have no subsidies, you've really got to tuck your sleeves up and work for what you want and that's what's saddening today. Farmers always had sidelines, a little shop . . . they never lived solely from the farm did they? Or the wife would keep guests in the house, somebody else would give teas, they all had a little sideline. Each fisherman had a pig or a cow, a piece of land whatever, something beside their farm to bring a bit in.

'We can see on television what happened on the mainland and we all have a love of nature naturally. We use a very, very tiny bit of pesticides, it's minute. We have so many flowers and butterflies, different flowers and butterflies that the tourists have never seen before. Just last summer the wild orchids were pointed out to me and someone said, "You have to go and dig it up," and I said, "No you leave it. It's grown there, you want to pick it up and put it somewhere else it's going to die, just leave it." I took the trouble to go and see where it was.'

'Channel Island people are accustomed to our cows and don't care for English beef. The fat part of our cows is yellow and of course the English want it white.'

'Set aside? That's an idea, we might as well turn Sark into a bird sanctuary. Tourism and farming don't compliment. We help one of the hotels out as much as we possibly can, we have done for years, but you see if we kept enough for what they wanted in the summer what would we do with the animals in the winter? Quite a lot of the hotels advertise all local stuff, one I know gets it all deep frozen from Guernsey. At one time there was talk about trying to send milk to the Guernsey dairies but by the time it would get there, and some days you couldn't get it there with storms. . . . I know farmers are always seen to be at the back of everything, blamed for this and that and the other, the point is that the labourer is getting paid more than the farmer makes.'

'The old say people were fitter and they're right. Different food, lived off the land, natural food. Now you see trailer, trailer loads of empty tins going down to the harbour, it was never like that. Two tins in a household a week. Now it's all tinned stuff, the big factories turn stuff out cheaper than the farmers can. I'm not worried about the future, I'm too old.'

43

*

'Things are getting difficult but there is a good future if people want to stick to it. This low-fat milk, well we've got to wave our flag to medical science about that, it'll pass, oh yes. A few years ago all the things you used to have they were so bad for you, well now they've changed round, other things.'

'To me, to be a farmer like I've done . . . I've been very, very fortunate because the wife, she was a farmer's daughter as well and it doesn't matter what we've come through the two of us we've always discussed things, even the crops we've put in different fields. At the moment I haven't been too good in health, my chest is my biggest problem and this [smoking] doesn't help. The point is it's my only vice really.'

# 4

## 'Look, Mummy. There's a pirate!'

One great advantage it derived from its isolation was that it escaped frequent outbreaks of plague which caused many deaths in neighbouring islands.

*(Fief of Sark)*

Yesterday was always better, tourists are not what they were. . . . The stereotypical day-tripper is flabby and sheep-like, a pale and middle-aged nonentity clothed in Crimplene who hesitates when faced with the choice of melon balls or soup. He wears his tour badge, behaves himself, his money in a zipped purse in his pocket. A timid man, frightened of adventure, his children miss the television set, hurl Coke cans, whine incessantly for sweets. But how can he prove himself, what can he do? The potential hero of the television disaster, the human bridge, the man who shouted 'fire!' – here on the Channel Islands, on his guided tour, he slumps and surrenders, shuffles on. His life is punctuated by the timetable not the tides. Should he run amok among the sea opaline jewellery or take a swing at the Sark sweaters with a broken bottle he might be late. His gesture, if he has one, is to drop a little litter, miss the bin.

Yesterday was always better, tourists made of sterner stuff. Happy days between the wars, families working as a team. Father had a knife in his sock and wasn't frightened to use it, mother kept the calomine, always wore a hat. Father blew up fifteen pneumatic cushions before breakfast, mother carried luncheon on her head. A whole day's excursion to a difficult beach, then back they climb singing 'Ten Green Bottles', children chewing happily on fish heads in those golden days pre-crisps.

45

A Craven A for father when they reach the top, a nip from the hip flask for Mother who, though only a woman, has done well. 'Discover Sark?' They certainly intend to and the *La Trobe Guide to the Coasts, Caves and Bays of Sark*, first published in 1914, will give them a hand up.

Stiff upper lips, backs like ramrods, good manners. 'Liquid refreshment for the boatman is seldom unappreciated.' 'Scrambling in bathing costumes is uncomfortable and unnecessary.' Rope-soled shoes, rucksacks, torches for the caves, tide tables, 'a study of the weather vane before setting out is rewarding. The sun's rays are very strong in Sark, and severe cases of overexposure are not uncommon.' To read *La Trobe* is to rediscover the lost world of the double negative, the deep water plunge, and bully-beef for luncheon – common sense, straight talking, encouragement:

> It should be said that while there is no danger in this scramble, there are two difficult points *en route*, which are more easily overcome if the party includes two or three agile men. . . . It is best to be frank, and for this bit over slippery rocks, with water all around about four feet deep, it may be said that the odds as to getting wet or not is an even money chance. We must now hurry back to make room for our friend – the tide.

And qualification:

> The reader, therefore, must not be put off when a scramble is described as 'difficult' or 'very difficult', the phrase merely signifies that a greater degree of care than usual should be exercised. In the majority of cases the worst that can befall is a ducking.

Those who scrambled with *La Trobe* in their back pockets might also have encountered Captain Platt. This Sark enthusiast of the same generation concludes his *Sark as I Found It* with fatherly advice:

46

The visitors do not and should not interest themselves in local politics. Why should they? Moreover, the Sarkee will certainly not discuss any grievance he may have, because the inhabitants are a silent people at the best of times. So long as you are content to pay their price for the hire of the boat to go round the island or fishing, that is all that is expected of you. Therefore I repeat, dear reader, gird up your loins and visit Sark for your holiday next year.


**Ballad of Cowardice** or (The Sark Dilemma)
At Fontaine Bay it's far too breezy
The tide is wrong for Vermande
At Havre Gosselin the water's greasy
The Sun has left Rouge Terrier
Where shall we have our bathe today?
Is it to be or not to be?
I think the sky is turning grey!
Let's go to the Sablonnerie.

Deribble Point is far from easy:
Greve de la Ville is hardly gay:
The Convanche ledge makes Mabel queasy
And Harold hates the Autlets;
At Jument rocks get in the way:
On Brechou we should miss our tea:
The trippers swarm in Dixcart Bay:
Let's go to the Sablonnerie.

I'm getting old: my breath is wheezy
My joints are stiff: my tendons fray;
The wind is cold: I'm feeling sneezy,
Perhaps there's fever in the hay;
Grand Greve is where the children play,
The little bastards bother me:
We can't get down to Port es Saies,
Let's go to the Sablonnerie.

*Envoi*
Princess of Sark, the isle is full:
The moonbeams shower upon the sea:
The point is – who leads whom astray?
Let's go to the Sablonnerie.

(H. S. MACKINTOSH,
quoted by kind permission of
Richard La Trobe Bateman)

Happy days between the wars. 'The perfect rest cure', 'Wonderful hospitality', 'Every comfort and attention', comments from the long-dead pressed between the marbled covers of the Visitors' Books from the Dixcart Hotel which go back to 1924.

The Misses S. from Regent's Park, travelling together – pressed, propositioned perhaps, by a lizard in the lounge? The Captain from the 52nd Light Infantry, Rawalpindi – dines alone? The couples from Bulawayo, from Penang – make up a bridge four? A family who give a temporary address of the Hotel Washington, Curzon Street – forced to share a table with some bounders from Bombay? 'First class', 'Wonderful service', 'Honeymoon (very nice)'. Ices in the garden for the children who've palled up, yesterday's children from 'Cyclops, Sittingbourne', 'The Chestnuts', 'The Haven', 'Two Elms'. . . .

Smitten by Sark families come again and again from 'Two Chimneys', 'Four Winds', and 'The Paddock', and the famous, incognito perhaps – Hugh Walpole '90 Piccadilly', July 1932, Philip Larkin, David Niven, Mary Quant. . . .

'I can remember people coming as far back as 1926. They travelled with trunks in those days. It was hard work running a guest house, they used to bring their silver with them, everything. I know one family who brought their own carriage to Guernsey. The guests would come every year for ever, they used to leave their bathers and rubber shoes in the house for next year. You knew who was coming, same bookings year after year. I remember Mr L.P. came to Guernsey on a mail boat and brought his nannies with him.'

Some visitors are diffident – flabby sheep? – remarks are not filled in unless more daring souls have already struck out at the top of a pristine page. A red Biro line marks the anthropologist's watershed, 'Under German Occupation from here'. Back they come in 1946: 'No austerity here!', 'Five weeks of Elysium', 'Superlative Honeymoon', 'Wizard Holiday'. Postcards home:

**Sark Alphabet Postcard**. Copyright E.W.P.

A are the Autelets, altar shaped rocks,
B the Boutiques, where the smugglers kept stocks;
C is the Coupée, sheer down to each sea,
D's Derrible, Terrible if spelt with a T.
E the Eperquerie, gorse trimmed by sheep,
F Fontaines, close by, going down to it's steep:
G is the Gouliot, choose a low tide,
H Havre Gosselin, you see from inside;
I are the Islanders called the Sarkese
J Just as much as they do when they please;
K are your Knees which will tremble and shake
L if from the Cave of Lament poor drowned souls should awake;
M is for Mouton, right down Jument's bay,
N is for nobody missing the way,
O are the Orgeris, Heaven and Hell,
P Pott, Little Sark – go there as well.
Q is the question: Should we take a whole day?
R Reply: Have you, did you, take much away?
S is the Seigneur's sweet garden of rest;
T Tintangue's handy, the afternoon best;
U is undressed as the goddess has seen us
V and she's plenty to choose from her pool that's called Venus,
W Bother now! What stands for W?
  I've done it in one line and therefore won't trouble you.
X the Unknown who has written this line,
Y he don't know and he hasn't the time;
  But has come to an end, and, as no one is dead,
  Well he's certain of this: That he's Z what he's zed.

It is at the Colinette that the day-trippers, exhausted by
their climb up the harbour-hill, come to a halt, mop their
brows and inquire which way to go. It is usual to send
them down the dipping path to the south, which leads
eventually to a small, rather ordinary bay. There they find
themselves in a stone pocket and as it is too much trouble
to trudge back to the main body of the island, they spend
the day wondering why they ever came to Sark.

(MERVYN PEAKE, *Mr. Pye*)

Early morning, May 1988. A sense of lull before the storm. A
cigarette and a cup of coffee at the Da San Café where Bessie is
preparing lunch for ninety day trippers on a package tour.
Seasoned holidaymakers, at the top of the tourist hierarchy, those
who come to Sark again and again and again, shop early. Their
bread is ordered and their names, for this fortnight at least, are
known. They cycle by, lettuces in plastic bags bouncing in their
bicycle baskets, into the village and out again before the rush.

Carriage drivers, up since 8.00 to feed and groom the horses,
collect in a gaggle outside the glass doorway of the new
supermarket, fortify themselves with packets of crisps and cans of
Coke to get them through the first 'load'.

The Sark Perfumerie is open now and 'The Little Shop'. The
island holds itself in readiness for the arrival from Guernsey of the
11.00 boat.

At the corner of La Collinette and Rue Lucas a signboard of
things to hire has already been set up:

> Baby Buggies £2.00,
> Fishing Rods £2.50 (includes bait)
> Umbrellas £1.00

and outside the little gift shop on Rue Hotton:

> Sark Jumpers. £4.99.
> Small, medium, large and Ex. large.
> Unisex. Six colours. The ideal gift.
> Don't miss our sea-opaline jewellery.

A boy stacks bikes across the road:

'We put about two hundred out, I began here when I was ten. It's a children's job, not a really drastic job. Get the bikes in and get them out again, put the money in the bank and keep so much out a week for dashing about with. Eight and a half hours a day. You can't hire bikes on Sundays but the boss'll open specially just for ten minutes if people have to bring bikes back. Accidents? Not many. The ones we get are fairly minor, nothing drastic, I mean nobody's been unconscious, died or any of that, some fall off and graze their elbows. We had one bad one once – he was going down the Coupée which he shouldn't have done anyway, and you know the concrete, he came off on there and broke his arm and his leg, he had to go to Guernsey! Saddles get eaten by horses, what is funny are the names, 'Admiral', 'Mr. Wally', 'Mr. Crap' – you've got to go into the backroom, that's why it was built I think, to stop yourself laughing.

'People from Guernsey, Jersey, English, French, Norwegians and Germans, Americans, about two Aussies every three months, not a common breed over here. The French are the most awkward, they want this bike not that one because the seat's too high. Do I speak French? Well if I was dumped in the middle of it I could get my way out of it. The Swedish and the French are the worst litter louts ever known, they just chuck it on the floor, it usually gets picked up by other visitors. The island keeps the streets cleaned, gutters get swept, horse dirt gets picked up all the time, there's a school-leaver doing it, paid by the island.'

There could be no argument that tourism created jobs, said the Archbishop of Canterbury, Dr. Robert Runcie, but 'the real value of those jobs may be less certain. It may be socially undesirable and even personally demeaning for young people to be trained only for jobs that are low paid, insecure and which carry inevitable overtones of servility.'
(LONDON CONFERENCE ON TOURISM, 1988)

## 'Battle of the bikes is a Sark shocker'

Bikes are big business in the Channel Island of Sark (three miles by two), where cars are banned and Shanks's Pony can be a bit wearing after a while.

So when Mr. Rossford de Carteret decided to set up Isle of Sark Cycle Hire (address, 'Behind the Belair pub') in competition to John Jackson's Jackson Cycle Hire it was a signal for all-out war.

Jackson, whose cycles had dominated the scene for years, engaged a small delinquent army of juveniles with an offer they could hardly refuse: £1.00 for every two de Carteret tyres they punctured and £1.50 for each buckled wheel, with bonuses for removing bicycles from circulation altogether.

The army set to with a will. Last year Mr. de Carteret, 43, lost ten of his original stock of 30 bicycles, which cost him £100 each.

This year he increased his stock to 150 – and the heat of battle intensified as well. He lost ten last month alone.

Then on Monday a woman tourist alerted the island constable when she saw three children making off with her hired bicycle while she was buying some stamps.

The constable called in reinforcements from Guernsey and Jacksons's street campaign was uncovered.

Things then moved swiftly. On Tuesday the magistrate Mr. Laurence de Carteret (no relation to the cycle firm) convened a special court in Sark school and yesterday Jackson was languishing eight miles away in Guernsey jail.

Jackson, who is in his fifties, admitted theft of a bicycle and an alternative charge of taking a bicycle without consent. He was shocked when the magistrate jailed him for a month, plus a fine of £300. His firm is now being run by a manager.

Mr. de Carteret, his competitor, said: 'The only problems we normally get are drunks. They take the bikes, ride them to the harbour at the bottom of the hill and leave them or throw them into the hoggins.'

He added; 'I am not a man to bear a grudge, though. Every time a bike goes missing I simply buy one more.'

(*Daily Telegraph*, August 1987)

'I'm so grateful that I knew those early years, that I knew Sark as she was. Quite a number of the visitors who came year after year well they gradually stopped coming because they ceased to find what they'd always gone for. Sark has been swept along. The Sark that I loved, that I fell for when I first went was the old Sark. There were no bicycles tearing about everywhere, no hiring of bicycles at all. Bicycles have become the menace of the island. The last time I went we walked on some of the cliff paths and I remember walking from La Manoir to Stocks Hotel, "ting, ling, ling," I thought, "It's never my Sark!" You'd have never seen a bicycle on the path, they'd have been on the roadway. Bicycles, hoards of them now.'

> Drawn up on the quay I saw what at first glance appeared
> to be a Bank Holiday parade awaiting the arrival of
> Queen Victoria. There, amongst the knots of people and
> the nets and lobster pots drying in the sun, was an orderly
> procession of hire carriages, all spruced up with drivers in
> their Sunday best, whips in hand, ready and willing to
> take anyone to any accessible spot of the island.
> (LEONARD CLARK, *Island of 100 Bays*)

'Carriages don't go down to the harbour any more, unless it's a royal visit. We have to be at the top of Harbour Hill by ten. We stand by our horses' heads and look appealing, actually it's rather daunting. Most times we don't get our first tour till eleven, by that time we've seen all the people that come off the boat and we've got enough to go round.'

The tourists are drawn up from the Harbour by the Sark bus, an open trailer with benches pulled by a tractor, known locally as the Toast Rack. Holding little leaflets provided by Sark Shipping Company, 'Discover Sark', they get off the bus and, let off the tour leash for an instant, stand as if spilt and unable to recollect themselves. They are unsure and look towards the woman in a tight blue suit and high heels with a yellow badge like theirs.

A little further up the hill stand the victorias and wagonettes. The drivers backing 'Trudy', 'Trixie', 'Trident' and 'Timmy', stars of a thousand photo albums, talk amongst themselves, hardly giving the newly arrived tour party a look.

Though in theory the carriage owners have a natural monopoly on the island and could combine to their advantage, they prefer to compete rather than co-operate and individual deals are struck with the tour operators. The drivers, mostly girls, are well wrapped up in old jumpers and anoraks and unlikely, in this weather, to suffer from burnt hands or the combination of wind and sun (and drink?) that produces 'carriage driver's nose'. They are 99 per cent outsiders, drawn to the island through ads in *Farmers' Weekly* and *Horse and Hound*, and very much form a group, hale and rather hearty with a reputation, not hard to come by on an island, of having too much of a good time. After ten days' training they have to pass a test on their knowledge of the island before they can take passengers on their own.

'Carriage drivers – they make a lot of it up. Out of the whole lot only one Sark man driving a van, all the remainder are young girls come out of Noah's Ark. It amuses me. Somebody came once and they asked the driver about Pilcher's Monument and the driver told them it had been knocked down, he took them up to Coupée and they could see the monument from there. It's the blind leading the blind.'

'Personally I think the worst of it is having so many boats now. In the old days we had a boat leaving Guernsey at ten, staying here the day and leaving here at five. I mean people had more time, the carriages had more time to take people around. A carriage ride cost 2 shillings and 6 pence a head. After the people had come up the Harbour Hill, within half an hour they'd dispersed. Agreed there wasn't the amount of shops there are now in the Avenue but they'd soon get dispersed and apart from seeing them at the Harbour Hill after they'd come in the morning and had a cup of tea, cup of coffee or a drink at the Belair, they were off until four, another cup of tea. They dispersed here there and everywhere.'

'A lot of the booked tours, because they have so many people coming over at one time, they like to try and fit three trips in so many hours. A trip should take about two hours and go right around the island. We go to the Coupée, to the Pilcher Monument, to the Eperquerie and the Seigneurie and the church. Instead of going right round by the mill some just go through the church to the Avenue. Their trip takes less than an hour and these poor people, a lot of them want to go and see the Coupée and half are having to walk down there. A long trek for those who've got children and if they're old or something. I met two who were absolutely exhausted and the poor little boy was white, he was pale because of the heat. I had only one space left in my carriage and I was going to take the little boy up but the parents, they were very annoyed about the trip. A lot of people feel they're being slightly cheated. Okay, it's slightly cheaper but it says they are seeing the whole island but they're not.'

> Host reactions to the apparent urgency of the tourist to
> experience as much as possible in a short time eventually
> may become exploitative. As they continually provide
> tourists with simplified and condensed experiences of their
> area, hosts may develop a dual price and service system,
> one price and quality of service for the tourist and another
> for fellow residents.
> (EMANUEL DE KADT, *Tourism: Passport to Development?*)

I ride in the Sarkee's carriage with four children, my sister and two Australian women who are periodically followed on bicycles by two Australian men.

'This used to be the Midland Bank that opened once a week on Mondays, if there was no boat we sometimes had to wait a fortnight before the clerk would come. Hey Rosie!

'The new telephone exchange. I preferred in my old-fashioned way the other one. If I wanted Tom, Dick or Harry on the blower . . . one minute on the blower in the olden days and I knew all the gossip. Now I know nothing.'

Our driver must be in his late seventies. Like a Russian guide he gives us what he thinks fit for our ears, he is friendly but keeps a distance between us and won't be drawn. It is rather like being taken around by an avuncular estate agent.

'This is the farm that was bought for £250,000, not the farm, just the property, about one acre of land. The price in 1920. . . . Fifty years ago the shipping company charged 3 shillings and 6 pence to come to Sark and the man who bought this house he thought he'd have a go. He tried 1s 6d and he ran his boats for a few years before he went bankrupt. He bought a lifeboat. He had a model cowshed and he had electric machines and a separator, then he bought the Ramsgate lifeboat and he tried his hand at the shipping. He converted it to take passengers then he had to sell. He bought another house and made himself a nine-hole pitch and putting course, he played golf with his friend General Haley but the General died about eight years later. With no one to play golf with he sold the whole lot for £15,500.

'We're long-lived here, the houses have long leases but they're considered short. After sixty-three years a man may come back and say, "I'm sorry but that's the end of your lease." Long-lived, the grandfather and the grandmother here died nearly a hundred. This freehold property. All three died. One man claimed this side and bought that lovely house, the other one was not claimed by anybody so the Seigneur owns it. Nice to be a Seigneur. Any property being sold the Seigneur takes his treizième, every thirteenth of the price. Maison Pommier was sold the other day for £220,000. You there, you want a sweet? We'll have to shorten the trip I'm sure. Now Paul McCartney, he's been after a place on Little Sark. How many people on the island? Five hundred, I don't know them all. Ask me that question years ago I would have said yes but now newcomers and the old ones are dying off like vegetation. More years ago there were twenty-eight pupils in my boys' school, just after the war so many went away.

'This is Cachemaille's Belfry. Everybody got very busy in Sark and they all made tapestry covers for the seats in the church. Also the recreation hall was built in 1927, there was a rifle range, nine-pin skittle alley, dance hall, cards and a library, it had its own electric clock with a heating system right through the hall. I helped knock down the old chapel for it to be built up here. "How many dead ones have you got in your cemetery?" one tourist asked me! That house, if you go in that house it's like going in Windsor Castle. £6,000 before the war, a millionaire bought it. In the sixties was the Jellicoe Plan, a landscape plan telling us what to do and what not to do. About where to build and about planting trees. The plan was not accepted. I thought, planting trees, that was a bad idea for me. I'm taking tourists round the island I want them to be able to see. Plant them in clusters . . . we lost a lot of trees during the Occupation.

'The island of Brechou, a bit of money, three quarter of a million pounds. The Dame sold Brechou to this man in 1927. The first thing he did was to use a helicopter and we didn't like the idea nor our tourists didn't like it, more so than us but anyway. . . . I proposed in the parliament against him having one, seconded by my friend and we had a special evening session of Chief Pleas so he did come over and we said we didn't mind him using the helicopter on Brechou, but he must never fly over Sark or land on Sark, ever. But – any time we wanted emergency that helicopter would be to our convenience so we told him that would be a good idea. The silly point is now that he has let the island to his secretary on a long lease. He's got a son, the heir should have it to vote.

'The Eperquerie. If you wish to walk down that little path with your cameras only, beautiful view. In the olden days we used to tell our tourists to be careful with LiLos. A woman, she knew better. She dozed off on this LiLo and the next thing she found herself floating away, somebody spotted her, halfway to France to land with no passport.

'I helped to build the Gallery, the artists' studio. I've read Mervyn Peake's book, *Mr Pye*. I'm half way with it, I'm not bothered to finish it. When they made the film they gave everybody on the island a barbecue in the evening, a good food feast.'

*

We stop at the Seigneurie and all troop out to look at the gardens. Whilst we're away I give the driver the recording I've made of our journey thus far, a sort of burglar public relations exercise. I show him how to play it back but something goes wrong, so that, listening to it months later, I'm confused by an unexplained and lengthy recording of him whistling 'Ave Maria'.

'We take the cart track, a short cut from Beauregard across the fields, to the road to the Coupée and Little Sark.

'We have bore holes on the island now, plenty of baths for the hotels, Cleopatra. . . . No sloes yet this year, some years they are very plentiful. That Pilcher Monument was put up here as a warning to you and I not to leave in stormy weather. 1868, some merchants from London and they wanted to come to Sark for a holiday you see with their private yacht. So one day they did arrive in Guernsey. Together with two Guernseymen they set sail from Sark, that afternoon, lunchtime, they were having lunch aboard the yacht then all of a sudden the thunderstorm arose and the wind was quick and the boat capsized and all lives were lost. Now this house here has double glazing, that's a house I'd like to live in in a storm. I built my house, my daughter's house, this house here the horse trough was too high for the dog so we put in a drinking bowl for him.

'Finally the Coupée, meaning the cut on the cliff. When my ancestors came here it was a deep gully, they couldn't take animals here, they made the causeway themselves. In the winter months heavy rain used to take all the rubble down the beach so, to stop that, the Germans put on a concrete surface and a railing.'

'I like to see people pass, in the winter it's dead to me. There's always a flow of people. I might be one of the rare ones, I prefer summer to winter. They're so busy in the summer and they haven't got time to breathe, that's what we say.'

A man with an anchor on his shirt, 'wrecked again', cycles down towards the Avenue: 'We've done the mill, lighthouse next.'

*

'Fines for leaving cycles outside this shop will now be 50p until September, all money to blind. The Water Carnival made £750. If we've missed anyone out please take this as a big thankyou from the Professor Saint Medical Trust.'

The comedian Tony Hancock would have loved the Mermaid Tavern, one can imagine him ending up here on a fun-filled day trip from East Cheam. The Mermaid down on Rue Hotton promises a 'live' group, 'Bathtime', on Saturday night, entrance £1.50. Inside, Spanish Galleon wallpaper, view of a beach that certainly isn't Sark – palm trees, sun, sand and a mountain. A very fat drunk in a fisherman's smock is holding court and winking at us from the bar. A shell ship's wheel light, wicker lamp shades, pool table and machines for holidaymakers in the rain. A couple sit with their heads in their hands. A clock made from half a barrel, anchors, mermaids and octupi in wrought iron on the bar. A wheel framing a sea view and multicoloured daisies; outside beheaded dahlias and bikes.

> Acculturation theory asserts that when two cultures come into contact of any duration each becomes somewhat like the other through a process of borrowing.
> (EMANUEL DE KADT, *Tourism: Passport to Development?*)

Dixcart Bay is Arctic. Seagulls race through the sky, white against the grey. A family of serious swimmers, bathing caps, stripes down the sides of their suits, swim lengths of the bay and look at their watches as they get out of the sea. Hunched against the cold I say, 'It's pretty near to heaven,' every time I light a cigarette.

The island is 300 feet up in places and Dixcart is the easiest walk down. All the beaches are stunningly beautiful, spotless, as God made them, not an ice-cream seller or an inflatable bouncy castle in sight. Port du Moulin, a harder climb near the north of the island, is spectacular. I stagger down behind an elderly woman who tells me she has just had a hip replacement. This is a headmaster's beach, rucksacks, sticks, hats, sandals with socks.

In the late afternoon English residents collect the one or two discarded Fanta cans and Mr Shine tins that their little boys threw stones at in the customary hour after lunch whilst waiting, impatiently, to go 'in'.

At Dixcart yachts lie at anchor in the bay. It's lunchtime and the sun's come out, the beach is almost empty apart from a small carousing group of New Zealanders who've come ashore in rubber dinghies and sunk their champagne bottle in the sand. They are joined by a disgruntled chef from one of the hotels plus his girlfriend. Further down the beach an Adonis lies on an orange motor launch, *Monkey Business*, he looks as if he has passed out but may be simply resting. I scribble in my sandy notebook, trying to get down what they say. Like someone with a poor seat at the theatre, I have to crane my neck uncomfortably to see what's going on. It's a pretty average play and, having arrived after the first act, hard to work out what relationship one has with another. The New Zealanders are very big, in swim suits positively hulking. God made them this size so that they could shoulder rucksacks. Their voices carry clearly across the empty beach, the champagne goes down fast and the talk is of drinking and hangovers.

'When even the toothbrush doesn't know you, you know you're in good shape.'

'The chef keeps his end up with a supply of local knowledge; the others, it seems, have only sailed in for the day.

'It's cheaper on Sark to buy the bottle. The Sarkese are a bunch of alcoholics anyway. It gets to 100 degrees in the kitchen, cool things down with a soda syphon. They don't drink much, they just top up then they're off again, another day gone.'

'No stamina, eh?'

'A lager is 90p. Jesus Christ, that home brew, a third of the price and it knocks your socks off, her kidney packed up. . . .'

'If you're stuck for food, go through the nosebag. Try to get sober and find your way back to the boat.'

A portable phone rings, it's for the corpse on *Monkey Business* who's finally aroused by two cans from the Esky.

'The Brits cover themselves with sun block, then they wonder why they never get a tan.'

Fired by drink the chef decides it's time to take a stand: 'I'm going to say, "Look. This is what I'm going to do, what sort of plate do you want it on?" She won't even say good morning to me.'

'She says it to me,' says the girlfriend with the kidneys, 'but then I get a sideways look.'

'The younger staff today will "borrow" anything. If they make it through the season depends on how quickly they find a girlfriend. I had two of the biggest clouts last year, just brainless.'

More yachtsmen motor ashore. There's an argument going on and the wife is sulking, staring hard at her husband's back as he pulls the dinghy past the tideline.

'Fag now or when we get to the top?' asks the husband taking a pack of Benson & Hedges from the waistband of his trunks. 'If you leave the lifejacket in the boat it's your fault if it gets nicked, all right?'

The wife hurls the lifejacket into the dinghy and leaves it there suspended on one of its pointed, science fiction, breasts.

'Sark consists of one thing only. Its very beautiful coastline which hasn't been raped yet except by the yachts who really are wrecking it, the peace has gone but they're not there all the time. If the weather's foul they go away. In foul weather you can get the island back again.'

'We never went down to the bays, only to collect the vraic.'

Perhaps it was an advantage to be there in the winter, for we were literally the only visitors on the island that second day. We had not only Dun I, but later Peploe's beloved beaches too, all to ourselves. Yet the story is different in the summer: every day the ferries disgorge coachload after coachload of tourists on the island, then pick them up again after a few hours. The Abbey alone had more than 100,000 visitors tramping through its grounds and buildings last year.

The tranquillity that so many seek on the island is thus

punctuated with periods of frenetic tourist activity, the lulls always followed by storms and the islanders feeling themselves both invaded and on show. We discovered discarded Sunblest wrappers, a plastic diet lemonade bottle, and a Smirnoff vodka bottle near the cairn on Dun I; one of the two shops on the island, tragi-comically, is now equipped with a television surveillance system to deter shoplifters. The tourists 'come and go', says Peter Macinnes with understated Hebridean courtesy. 'They're being coped with.'

(ANDREW STEPHEN, 'IONA', *Observer Magazine*, 1988)

Considerably more is known about the economic benefits of tourism than the associated costs. Incremental, intangible costs, which are hard to measure and may be overlooked until major, irreversible changes in society or the environment occur.

(EMANUEL DE KADT, *Tourism: Passport to Development?*)

It is early in the season and in the Belair pub at the top of the Harbour Hill it is still quite possible to get a round. Inside locals play characters to the tourists who in this context are not allowed any character at all. Books on the sociology of tourism are not a good read for those who wish to be aroused from coma. Frankness is not its style: what a sociologist lurking in this bar would read into the 'interplay between hosts and visitors' is actually quite evident to the naked untrained eye. What happens at the Belair can be roughly translated as a meeting between characters and tourists who are reduced to a sort of non-being, a meeting between characters and nouns.

'We just enjoy Sark so much, it's so relaxed. Forget about all your worries and just have a lovely relaxing day. It's changing. It's still very different from anywhere else, it's still a lovely place, something very special. We hire a bike and we amble around, we sit and we just look out at the lovely view, up by the Pilcher Monument. Just the peace, just lovely, or at the very end of Little Sark.'

They come, an' they quit an' go on; an' every damn one of
'em's got a little piece of land in his head. An' never a
God damn one of 'em ever gets it. Just like heaven.
Ever'body wants a little piece of lan'.

(JOHN STEINBECK, Of Mice and Men)

'We'd like to live here really, give it a try. Just have a few cows,
couldn't come here with nothing to do. If you had another income
and just did farming as a hobby. . . . Whether we could come here
and make a completely new life and friends and feel as we did at
home I don't know . . . we've had friends with us whenever we've
come . . . the winter, that would be the trial period. We came in
the autumn once for the day. We couldn't afford to come here
without having to work and I'm sure farming here is a closed
shop, anyway you couldn't just rely on farming, you'd have to
have some other source of income. . . .'

Most winter evenings a few men gather in each bar. The
very manner in which they walk into the bar often
suggests a curiously subdued state of mind. The
newcomer greets those already at the bar, asks for his
drink, and falls silent. Conversational exchanges between
drinkers are abrupt and cursory. There is rarely any
ongoing dialogue. Pauses between the few fragments of
dialogue are long. Each speaker hesitates so much for
thought, and anticipates so little by way of response or
reply, that his few words are often left suspended in the
bar's quiet too long for the next words to sound like a
reply. Indeed, the most frequent real reply is simple
accord, the familiar 'Ah, 'tis'. These men do not stay for
the long hours in the bars which characterize their
summer drinking nor do they often consume the sheer
volume of alcohol drunk in the summer. . . . The year can
now be characterized as elation in summer and
despondency for the rest of the year.

(HUGH BRODY, Inishkillane)

By early evening, and even for the writer it's a long day, the
carriages are back in barns and sheds, the horses out to grass. The

carriage drivers discuss their day, an event I join in with until the baby is frightened by a pig.

'"Must be nice living here, there's nothing to do," never realised how ignorant the public are. Come from Guernsey and they've got it all included in the package. . . .'

'I had someone on my carriage that told me everything. I nearly throttled her. She'd lived in Guernsey a year and she knew everything about Sark. She was a doctor's wife and I had Americans and they thought it was gospel what she was saying. We think of them as punters.'

'I worked at the Royal Mews before I came here, I didn't like London, this is more my scene. I go hunting with a dog, I like the country, I'm supposed to go to Texas for three months after this season. One of our phrases is, "in the real world". When you get to Guernsey it feels like a metropolis, 'it's not that here everything's so different, it's just things that people get away with here – they'd be killed for it on the mainland and yet on the other hand things that are so petty get blown-up out of all proportion.'

'It's dreadful at the top of Harbour Hill, one better than the other. You get your horse groomed, get them in, ride one and lead the others up the road but it's not easy walking them up the road because they all walk at different paces. A girl and boy came, they didn't know much about horses. The boy painted the carriages and the girl went to work in one of the hotels. We get Sunday off to sit on the beach, I haven't been to Guernsey since I arrived.'

'It's excellent here, like paradise isn't it? There are jobs maintaining the roads in the winter but I think it would get stale if you stayed here all the time. We've got a television that heats up after five minutes and people have white hairdos and the screen goes nearly all white so you just have to listen to the television.'

'It's interesting and different. In some ways it's easy because you just sit on the carriage and do nothing but when you've done two and perhaps maybe doing a third trip and you're talking and the words just keep coming out, and out, and out, it ends up . . . just sort of gets repetitive. Sometimes you get a grumpy lot, specially if they're booked, they haven't come up to your carriage and chosen you, and they aren't too happy. Sometimes it's difficult to remember what to say. They ask you what you do in the winter, sidetrack you and then you're going on about Chief Pleas or constables and you sometimes think, "Crikey have I said this before?"'

> A vacation for the tourist is a novel experience but its consequences for the host are routine.
> The tourist sees the country or destination visited in terms of its superficially picturesque, predictably exotic or typical aspects and experiences local life highly selectively and episodically. The shorter the stay, the greater the distortions of reality.
> (EMANUEL DE KADT, *Tourism: Passport to Development?*)

'Day-tripperwise tourism has reached saturation point without a doubt. The day-trippers, they just don't have time to see the real beauty of Sark. The only astonishing thing about that is you actually talk to them down at the harbour and back on the boat and quite a lot of them say they've had a lovely day and they come back. The carriage tour around the island has been cut down. Because there's so many coming over, they have a short tour and just tootle around The Avenue for the rest of the day. We've never really decided what we want from tourism apart from the cash. Our natural buffer-zone of Guernsey in between absorbs the impact, as it were, and they have got to get from Guernsey to Sark by sea which makes it so much harder. I think we're accommo-dating tourism about as well as anywhere I've seen, I mean, you go to some places it's ghastly – North Wales for example, they've got it down to a fine art there. . . . The tourist never sees the old

Sarkees, they don't know a real islander from, say, me, who's been here ten years.

'Look, Mummy. There's a pirate!'

# 5

# The Occupation

'During the Occupation my father wanted to get a message to La Dame and he heard that La Dame, "The Königin" as the Germans called her, wanted also to get a message to him. They met in the end by accident.

'"I wanted to speak to you," said my father.

'"And I wanted to speak to you," said La Dame.

'"You go first," said my father.

'"No, after you," replied La Dame.

'"I want to speak to you about fraternisation, Madame."

'"I want to speak to you about fraternisation," she replied.'

August 1988. Talking to old fisherman in the café at the top of Harbour Hill. A boat has just come in, it's raining and the café is absolutely full, loud with shunting china and other people's conversations. We sit sharing cigarettes and smiling, it's obvious that nothing either of us say will be picked up on the tape.

The place empties as the rain stops, the sound of laughter from the waitresses comes through the silence, the sight of men in uniform with machine guns on their backs. Neither of us have any idea what is going on and switch our attention to the bar of the café where just minutes ago the tourists were sliding trays of tea and coffee. A soldier, a marine, who speaks in broken English with the accent of Charles Aznavour after a heavy night, is trying to fix a date with one of the waitresses. All the girls giggle and preen. Outside the café we see at least eight more soldiers being inspected by an officer. They are French marines, come to lay a wreath and erect a new headstone, in homage to the unsuccessful Allied raid on Sark in December 1943.

Foreign accents, men in uniform, giggling girls,

'We were neither friends nor enemies with the Germans, that's the way I looked at it. We had to obey, there was no way out. Here they were all around us, there was absolutely no way out. You just did as you were told and if you did as you were told. . . . The ones I met were very kind. There were two Germans who used to come around here and took quite a liking to one of my daughters and of course, well, I didn't like it that much, you never know. . . . But it turned out that his daughter was the same age and he sort of adopted her as his own and his mother used to send him a little parcel, three little cakes, and he used to fetch them and bring them to my daughter, as they were, unopened. What do you say against people like that?'

The man who told me the story of his father and La Dame is anxious that I get to the truth. Julia Tremayne's Diary, *War on Sark*, is not the truth, he says. The truth has not been written, he insists, though *Islands in Danger*, by Alan Wood and Mary Seaton-Wood, comes near to it. He says I must find my way to the truth, that the way to do it is to listen to all sorts and get rid of the lies. When I ask him how I'll know a lie when I'm told one, he doesn't answer. Truth will apparently be something that hits me in the eye, like love, I'll recognise it.

> I don't believe that a period of history – a given space of time – my life – your life – that it contains within it one 'true' interpretation just waiting to be mined. But I do believe that it may contain within it several possible narratives: the life of Hugh O'Neill can be told in many different ways. And those ways are determined by the needs and the demands and the expectations of different people and different eras. What do they want to hear? How do they want it told?
> (BRIAN FRIEL, *Making History*)

> As far as possible we have confined our narrative to a series of facts without interpretation. Wherever two

68

separate versions of a particular story are both current and credible we have included both, not wishing to take sides in 'feuds' that still smoulder after 17 years.

(MICHAEL MARSHALL, Hitler Invaded Sark)

The more I have to do with facts the less attractive they become. There must be a Chinese proverb about facts on the lines of 'Go looking for a fish and your wok will remain empty'. Prospecting for facts and facts alone implies a tunnel vision reminscent of the law. The facts, the truth about Sark during the Occupation or at any other time, exist, if they exist at all, in the fictions, the anecdotes, the opinions, the asides.

Julia Tremayne was English, sixty-seven years old at the start of the Occupation, and lived with her daughter at Grand Dixcart which she ran as a guest house. Authentic or not, her diary is a monument to the small things, a diary about socks and hens and what she made soup out of, her dreams and her reality, the contents of her store cupboard. It bears some comparison to the fictitious *Journal of Mistress Joan Martyn*, written by Virginia Woolf in 1906. 'I shall store up fine linens & my chests shall be laden with spices & preserves; by the work of my needle all waste of time & use will be repaired & renewed.' As Lyndall Gordon writes in her book, *Virginia Woolf: A Writer's Life*:

> Joan's journal is a document which her male descendants assumed to be insignificant. . . The centre of history is not the legal document or the muddled vicissitudes of the Wars of the Roses but the woman left alone in her citadel, who kept order as a matter of course, who kept anarchy, so far as she was able, at bay.

Without the Tremayne journal stories about the Occupation are isolated, roll in the palm like single beads; Tremayne gives us at least a sense of the whole necklace, of how it felt to wear that necklace round your neck.

The Diary is rich in detail, rich in fear: the price of eggs; the art of barter; 75 shillings for a pound of tea; a ukelele and a tennis racquet swapped for hen food; deals struck in the Exchange columns of the Guernsey paper; a wedding dress for a bag of sugar. Giving and lending, reading old newspapers, swapping books, darkness: 'England summertime plus one hour German time equals all night and no day.' Going to bed in the dark with one candle; the noise of machine-gun practice; planes overhead; the wreckage in the bays that no one will collect, 'The sea must be full of dead bodies now.' Bottling tomatoes, making jam, living on potatoes, the cry of bloodhounds, the language of the little lanes – 'Italian, French, German, Patois, Polish, English, Austrian' – the sound of children singing in German, the sight of children aping German soldiers. It catches what historians, writing after the event, can't catch, the reckless arithmetic of rumour.

Gossip, speculation, fear. 'Wireless confiscated!' A Peace Ball mooted for August 1940 when Germany would have conquered England. Hope, May 1941, 'Only a few months more.' In August 1944 she unearths the Union Jack, in September she folds and puts it away again.

Rumours and counter-rumours, exclamation marks. Typhus and diphtheria in Guernsey, paper bandages, people dying in the streets. 'All British born are to be evacuated. Too many mouths to feed. I won't go!' Her desperation and bouts of near hysteria come down to us like the village cries of England in the plague years, 'God is Deafe!' They may reflect little more than the diarist's personality, but the lasting worth of this disputed document must be the tedium of occupation discerned between the lines. The stillness and the periods of silence, the sense of being closed in on the island, bad enough in peace time:

> At times the gales surrounding the island became so insistent that one longed for silence, the uncanny silence which sea-mist carries, but the eerie sound of fog-horns was a poor substitute for it.
> There were moments when I particularly felt an intense claustrophobia, knowing that in whichever direction one went there was the sea, and one was trapped.
> These feelings did not last very long, although there

70

were times when no boats could come from Guernsey with provisions or mail for a week or two at a time.
(MAEVE GILMORE, *A World Away: A Memoir of Mervyn Peake*)

During the Occupation no boats came and perhaps they would never come again. As an eighty-year-old who spent the war on Guernsey told me, 'It wasn't the starvation, it was the uncertainty.'

July 1940 was dry, a wonderful year for the roses. On 3 July a lifeboat arrived at Creux Harbour bringing about ten German soldiers and a corporal. This was the beginning of the Occupation of Sark, which was to swell the population by hundreds and lasted until 8 May 1945.

'Oh, they were hard days, hungry days, especially for the children. Mine for instance, they were all between fourteen and eighteen, you know that age, they were the hungry age I always thought. We gave them mostly vegetables but then what is there in vegetables without a piece of pork to have some fat? You see there was just nothing and they just went through them. But we were lucky in a way, we had two cows and naturally we had a bit more milk and butter than those that didn't but then we had to give a certain amount to the Germans out of that lot. That was ever so funny. Well, this will tell you how some of them were really good. So as to eke out the milk so that everybody would have a bit more the Sark people had good milk but the German stuff was watered-down. My hubbie used to have to work for the Germans, everybody who had transport had to work for them, he had a horse and a wagon. He used to have to take the soup out to Little Sark, wherever their barracks were, and the day before – all depended which farmer's milk they were taking – he would say, "Careful tomorrow boys, the inspector's coming," and of course that day and the following day the milk was very nice! I think they knew, they must have, I mean you don't get milk one colour one day and a different colour the next. Some say the German troops went into the fields at night and milked the cows but I don't think so. I think they'd have been too scared of the commandant.'

71

'The mill stopped grinding in 1921 or '23, then we had our flour from Guernsey, but during the Occupation they had a grinder in the Seigneurie grounds. It was a powered job, you know, and they used to grind the flour there. We were rationed so tight all the farmers grew the wheat and you were allowed 10 per cent of what you grew, the remainder had to go to the island depot to feed the population of Sark. The farmer himself, through his pains whatever, he used to earn his 10 per cent extra and you would take it to the Seigneurie and they would grind it for you. It wasn't pure white as it is now but it was very, very good bread and as we were farmers we used to bake our own bread once a week. You could either have your full ration of flour or your bread. We used to bake our bread in a furze fire, a furze oven at La Tour Cottage. It had this oven and we used to bake our bread once a week, burning gorse, we used to bake every Wednesday. The bread that was made on the island in the bakehouse – I'm not saying it wasn't good, it was good with what he had to play with – but we had our 10 per cent more. On a farm we had more and that's why Sark survived better than Guernsey or Jersey, nobody died of starvation here. If it happened now it wouldn't last six months, the modern housewife today wouldn't know how to make a meal together. We were never without bread on Sark but Guernsey and Jersey were six weeks without bread, an awful long time without bread. That lovely vegetable market in Guernsey, I have seen it myself and all they had was potato peelings for sale. I think it's like anything else, you find a way out because you're trapped.'

1941. The island no longer belongs to us. They are laying mines and barbed wire over cliffs and bays, we are real prisoners in a cage.

(JULIA TREMAYNE, *War on Sark*)

Hundreds of thousands of mines were laid.

'Do you know what happened once? Up at the Mermaid there were mines and an old man that was a bit gone in the head by then, he walked right through the minefield and the Germans were there watching him and they saw him. Somebody was going to shout to him but they said not to say anything and, blimey! he did it. If they'd shouted, he would have changed his course, he went right through the minefield, he didn't know.'

'All the cliffs were mined, I found one, years later in the bay. There were some visitors in the bay, children, and I didn't want to leave it where it was for the sea to take it out again so I went to the woman and I said, "Take your children and go to the other side of the bay." I said, "There's a mine here and it could go off if I touch it." The mines were supposed to be more dangerous than when they were new and I said, "I'm going to move it so if anything happens you must report what happened," and I picked it up, I can tell you I could hardly put my feet down! I moved it to the top of the beach then I told her, "Now. The path is clear," so I notified the constables and they blew it up.

'There were some mines left in the bushes. One afternoon we were lifting potatoes in the next field and we threw something in and the one that went off lifted up two others. I'd been hunting with my dog in those bushes. . . . The land mines were about the size of a two-pound jam pot and mostly packed with little steel marbles. It was really impossible to walk through if you didn't know.

'The man who laid the mines stayed for the whole Occupation and I watched him rabbiting between the mines one day. I noticed what he did and I got up early and I had a couple of rabbits. But most of the Germans didn't know where the mines were. There was one fellow, I didn't like him, he shot a rabbit in the cliff by the house, in the minefield. I knew where they were because we used to watch them put them in you know, they were half-way down the cliff.

'I have never been able to understand it really . . . two sheep got loose and they were chained and they went across the minefield and it didn't explode, really. I still had some sheep on the stake then and two of them got loose, dragging their chains. Of course their feet are so small, but what puzzled me was the

73

weight of the chain. Perhaps it needed a certain weight to set the mines off, I don't know. Tiny little square mines, not supposed to kill but to maim, there were hundreds in the field. The Tommies made sure that they were all gone but they used to get the Germans to lift them then they made the German prisoners march up and down to make sure. But I was worried until the first time I had that field ploughed again, I can tell you!'

October 4th, 1944. A little girl was killed yesterday, only four years old. She strayed onto a minefield just in sight of her own house. Two cousins near her were badly wounded with shrapnel. I wonder there have not been dozens of deaths before now, for we expected coasts to be mined but not up to our back and front doors.
(JULIA TREMAYNE, *War on Sark*)

'There was only one that had it with the mines and that was a little girl, she was the same age as my son. Well, the mines weren't properly covered and she was going to see her father who was digging potatoes in the field and she saw this shining, the top of the mine was shining in the sun. She wasn't alone but she was the one that went. She must have put her foot on it turning to come back, she got it in the back of the head and the one with her, she got a scratch on the cheek. I saw her. The back of her head had gone.'

'The island was made very small and we couldn't go down to the bays, but Sunday afternoon they had Grand Greve, that was heavily mined, the path all the way down, but Sunday afternoon they'd remove those mines so that we could go down with our families. We did go, grateful to get away, yes, but again you had to feel that it was nice of them if you like. I mean they could have just not bothered about us but we thought it was, you know, good of them to shift the mines so that we could go down, there was no need for them to do it. I think we could also go down to that little beach at the harbour but of course when the raid came well, that just about did it. After the raid, the Dixcart Landing, everything was tightened up, everybody had to report at five o'clock at the Manoir, everyone from fifteen to ninety or something. All had to turn out and that landing, well it had nothing to do with Sark, eh?'

In October 1942 Geoffrey Appleyard led a commando raid on Sark:

> Appleyard had spent a holiday on Sark with his family some years before the war. They were somewhat mystified when, at home on leave, he ran through an amateur cinema film they had taken there: he was refreshing his memory of the place where they had stayed. He decided he would go ashore on the promontory known as the Hog's Back, on the south side of the island, and then cross the Dixcart Valley – avoiding Dixcart Bay itself, because he thought the beach was certain to be mined.
> (ALAN WOOD AND MARY SEATON-WOOD, *Islands in Danger*)

The raid – in which four German engineers were shot and one prisoner taken – had serious repercussions, for Germany alleged that the dead had been shot by commandoes when their hands were tied:

> The handling of the matter by British propagandists can hardly be called happy. The first official statement on the raid merely said that 'Five prisoners were taken of whom four escaped after repeated struggles, and were shot while doing so.' Later Whitehall officially admitted that the hands of the prisoners on Sark had been secured. . . . 'The hands of the Germans were tied so that arms might be linked with the captors.'
> (ALAN WOOD AND MARY SEATON-WOOD, *Islands in Danger*)

German propagandists made much out of the raid, and on 18 October Hitler announced that henceforward captured commandoes would not be treated as prisoners of war but would be 'slaughtered to the last man'. On Sark it meant the beginning of a tighter regime, and resulted in deportation of many English-born islanders, a further loss of freedom of movement on the island, and an extension of the curfew.

The second and last raid took place in December 1943. The commandoes were trapped by mines. Two died, the others escaped, but all but one of them was wounded. The wreath brought to Sark in August 1988 commemorates these men:

A la mémoire du quartier Robert Bellamy qui repose ici et du soldat André Dignac du Ier BFM Commando. Morts pour la France au cours d'un Raid de reconnaissance préparant la Liberation de l'Europe.

Another tombstone reads:

Koninkrijk der Nederlanden
D. Brusselman Bootsman KM
25.7.1906 – 1.5.1941

'It happened I was Constable for the first, second year of the Occupation, I had a bit of fun out of it. There was a corpse found down at Havre Gosselin. Of course I had to go. Two German soldiers were down there, fixed bayonets, hand grenades, the lot. . . . "What the bloody hell do you think you're doing?" I asked them. "This man is already dead."

'It was a person from the Netherlands Navy, either Belgian or Dutch, I've got some of his brass buttons. I always thought he went down at Dunkirk, he had been three months in the water, he had two life-belts still on, there was only the skull, the flesh was coming through his clothing. They wanted to undress him, I said, "Not likely! You're not undressing him, he died from the cold, drowning." He had a lovely full set of teeth, he was a young man, he still had an identity disc on his wrist, when they took it off his hand came off. One of his buttons rolled on the floor of the shed so I put my foot on it, and his watch.

'They told me it was my responsibility now to bury him. I went straight to the Manoir and asked for the permit for the carpenter to be able to work overnight and we buried him the following day and the German officer came to the funeral and saluted him. They weren't all bad, there were some good ones. We were told after that they'd broadcast to either Belgium or Holland that he was being buried. He was a petty officer, they sent his stripes to Holland.'

> If anything could be thought amusing in those days it was the German effort to control our fishing. They were so afraid that fishing boats might escape and reach England that an armed soldier was placed in each boat. . . . The Sark fishermen amused themselves by deliberately steering the boats into large waves, watching the German guards getting well soaked and often sea-sick, and staying out much longer than was necessary for the pleasure of watching them get sicker and sicker.
> (DAME OF SARK, *Autobiography*)

'Germans came with us but we never spoke about the war. We fished, we spoke about his home, family, some of them knew English, it was no good if you didn't. I'd a very good one in our boat, he had a letter from his wife, he'd read it, tell us how they were and his children. He had a home life same as we did, he was called that's all, called to colours and he had to do it. I think they were lonely, what is life without women? Mind you they were pretty decent, they didn't bother the girls much, five years, of course when you look at it, it's nature isn't it? They took 10 per cent of the fishing but they paid in German money, some didn't think the money was worth anything after the war but it was.'

> February 1st, 1942. We have a bowl of early primroses on the table, so it tells of spring. I begin to feel like a 'wandering minstrel', a 'thing of shreds and patches'. We darn and patch and unpick and reknit all day long.
> (JULIA TREMAYNE, *War on Sark*)

'The war mucked us up and after it we really wanted to get away, confined so long on top of the island, loads of restrictions. What I longed for was a really smart shoe. . . . A lot of us didn't wear shoes, in the summer anyway. The German doctor said it was better to go barefoot. Because we had run a guest house before the Occupation we had plenty of linen and blankets. Men's shirts were made out of curtains and bedspreads and I remember we three girls had blanket coats and the button holes done in different coloured Sylko, red and green. Then there were things to be had at the Seigneurie, you could go there for things. For toothpaste we used cuttlefish, scrape them to get the powder out and make it into a paste. We didn't know German money would be honoured after the war and we spent a lot of it. And we burnt all sorts of things when it was over. I remember making a bonfire, getting rid of everything to do with the war, ration books, identity cards – we were so fed up with carrying all that stuff around with us – I suppose we burnt a fortune? The war mucked us up. If the war hadn't come I would have liked to have been a nanny, to travel like kids do today, if I'd been brave enough.'

'If little Sark was invaded they would blow the Coupée up, that was the general idea, they wanted us off Little Sark. Everything was mined around here right up to the stables. Between the generator shed and X's house there was a tank there. They had their guard there and their gun emplacement and they had a watch there, it was their lookout. We couldn't get down to any of the bays. You could go to Guernsey but you had to have a permit, you had to have an excuse, a medical excuse. And also the same thing, if you wanted to knock down a tree to burn you had to have a written permit from the commandant.'

'We had no artificial food in those days and some of the war we didn't even have a doctor. There was a doctor at the end of the war but no one trusted him, but he was a damn good doctor. He used to make his own medicine, herbs from the hedges. Some people used to say he was a bit mad but he saved my wife's life. She was getting worse all the time so I went and fetched him and when I came back I really thought she was dying. The tablets she was taking were too strong. The doctor saved her. Illness was one way to get to Guernsey, they always had toothache.'

> We live in a dead world with no news, not much energy
> and easily tired, German lies in the paper.
>                                   (JULIA TREMAYNE, *War on Sark*)

'You never knew one day to the next what was happening. Of course we did get the news but we weren't supposed to get the proper news. There was a Cypriot over here, captured by the Germans, he used to make crystal sets.'

'There was a little crowd in Guernsey, one of them worked for the *Press* and they listened to the British news and they started *GUNS, Guernsey Underground News*. My husband was one of those. The man who worked for the *Press* used to print all this, you see, and one week one of us would receive this letter and my husband the next week. It terrified me, I thought perhaps he might be doing some good but at the same time it was very, very risky. I can see those letters now, it was always red ink, the address was always red. "Oh dear, put it away quick before someone sees!" It was horrible. I didn't know all that much about it, I wasn't told. It was only a few you see, the ones they could really trust, that they passed it on to. In the end the man from the *Press* was caught, you know, and he had a hell of a life, didn't he? In Germany, he died there actually, he was caught and that was through a friend of his, talking too much.'

'The children didn't mind, they didn't understand, did they? To children it was playing, you can't blame them. I remember my father being taken away, I walked behind them as they took him, singing. There were fourteen people in the house that day. . . .'

> Of all the islands we were in the best position to
> withstand occupation. We were 400 people, mostly able to
> produce vegetables. We had 103 cows, a few rabbits, some
> of us had poultry and others pigs. The men were either

79

farmers or fishermen so we had our own crops and our own fish. All had been well until we had been subjected to bureaucratic rules and regulations. The office workers in army uniform knew no more about farming and fishing than the islanders did about office work, nevertheless they gave numerous instructions as to what crops should be sown and how they should be grown.

(DAME OF SARK, *Autobiography*)

'As farmers it didn't have much effect on us except when they wanted your implements, they did a bit of growing to have food for themselves.

'If you weren't frightened of them you were all right. I remember once one of the officers came when I was harrowing my patch of oats, they wanted my harrow, I told them they couldn't have it, the seed was in the ground, but to them it didn't matter. The officer made a move to unharness my horse, I went mad! I knew how to handle a whip in those days, I thrashed it about an inch from his fingers and at the same time, in coming down the field, I cut a bramble from the hedge. I told the officer if he dared touch the harness his finger was coming off like that bramble. There was some Sark swearing I can tell you. I wasn't frightened, I didn't care. I should have because I had a wife and child but I was mad. "Why don't you go somewhere else, there's other harrows on the island. Go and ask Mrs Hathaway", she wasn't the Dame then, "and leave me in peace for a while. Your commandant tells us to grow stuff and here you are delaying us." I told them to get off my land and they went. The officer had a revolver, if they had ammunition . . . I don't know. I mean we were damn lucky not to get shot.'

'They didn't like it when you stood up to them really, especially the young ones. There was one, I'd just been separating milk and he wanted some milk. I said, "You're not having any milk, go and ask Hitler for some milk," he went a bit mad. I'd two buckets of skimmed milk to feed the pigs. I said, "You want some milk, that milk is for the swine not for you." I was sorry for him, he was starving really.

80

'One of them I used to give him a glass of milk, he did some work with the horses. My horse got lame, I think he put his foot in a rabbit hole, and we had him in the stable for three months and this German used to come every night to dress the wound. I didn't touch it, I used to go and fetch this chap, he cured it. Mind you the horse was in a state, he was only skin and bone. For the first three weeks you could see the horse steaming with pain, but the German cured it and I had the horse for years after. The first time I harnessed him he told me to go easy and I put him on the little plough and he wouldn't do the length of the field so I didn't force him. I stopped as soon as he stopped. Every day I harnessed him and every day he did a little more. No vets, no, but during the war the animals, they were like us, they didn't get sick. We could cope with milk fever, the old remedy with that, we used to pump up the udder, blow them right up until they were like a football.'

'We were four and a half years without tobacco, we had to smoke clover leaves. The Germans were rationed too but sometimes they would give you a fag. Oh but it was worse, if you taste a good fag and then . . . back to clover leaves, oh! We had it in the back of our minds all the time, we're the winners, no matter what, we're going to win. Some said that England had forgotten us but, when you look at Sark, only a small population, they knew we had enough.'

'There was a very short chap, he was a bugger, towards the end of the war. I know they were hungry. . . . He walked straight in, he wanted some bread. I said, "Get out," and this fellow, he used to make more noise with his boots than the whole bloody regiment. I heard him stamping, he opened the back door, I said, "Here's that little so and so again!" I got up from the table and I met him in the kitchen doorway and I caught him by the throat and I put him outside.

'"I want bread."

'"You're not having any bread. If you come tomorrow you're *kaput!*"

'I was facing him in the yard, and he was a very short chap, I was facing him and shaking my fist under his nose and I gave him my boot in the backside and I let him go and I said, "You return and you're finished!" and he never came back again.

'And it happened when they came with the prisoners of war to do the work – at the end of the war, you know, they made the Germans clean up their own stuff – I was going down to the harbour and I happened to spot him and I said to the Tommie, "You see that little bugger, well kick his arse and don't stop!"'


In January 1945 a Red Cross boat brought food parcels to Sark.

'Chocolate, cigarettes, tea, coffee, biscuits. Did we have flour? Butter, cheese, oh it was wonderful, everything we hadn't had for years, you see. We didn't know when it was going to end, it was always going to be next year. . . .'

'I remember hearing the news that the First World War was over, I was in Bolventor, Cornwall. I married a Sark girl during the second war, her parents didn't come, couldn't come to the wedding, we couldn't even have a photograph taken, there was no film. But we were allowed to get married and then, shortly after that I had to go to Guernsey to work for the Germans. They picked us out you see and I was an engineer, if they were labourers they didn't have to go. The Germans commandeered three motor cruisers and one German had to go out with the fishermen. We had three boats, two we used to have on the quay and we used to look after them and keep the engines running and switch over if they wanted it. Then we used to come back to Sark every fortnight. Then the Germans said they wouldn't have a boat for us to come back. November '42, the States of Guernsey had to find us accommodation. As long as she was with me it was all right, we had a flat in the main street opposite Woolworth's. When the end came I remember I was in the bathroom and I saw what was happening. I called to my wife and we went down to the Weighbridge, at the most there were fifteen people there.'

*

'I would have gone away but the war stopped it. We had no money, that was the beginning and the end. Dreams, we had such wonderful dreams. After the Occupation we couldn't get out quick enough. First job that comes along I'm going to take it kind of touch. I went to work on a big estate in England, Dorset. Never been on a plane or a train. I was met at Bournemouth. I went over there in October, I came home for Christmas, I had to change trains at midnight. The first night away was terrible. They all said I'd be home in a month but I stayed two years to show them. I jolly well won't come back, I thought, no matter how homesick.'

'After the Occupation I joined the Merchant Navy but then I came back. I still walk down to the Pilcher Monument, look out to sea, think about those days.'

'I always looked upon it, they were somebody's sons, they didn't want to be in the war, not the ordinary Tommy, you know, private. But of course when the *Vega* came, the Red Cross parcels and that, I wouldn't have given them not a bean because my way of thinking was that our sailors risked their lives to get here and it wasn't fair to share. We had to go to the island hall to collect our parcels and they never touched one of them, you know, and they were much hungrier than we were. . . .'

# 6

# *In Memoriam*

You have to begin to lose your memory, if only in bits and pieces, to realise that memory is what makes our lives. Life without memory is no life at all. . . . Our memory is our coherence, our reason, our feeling, even our action. Without it we are nothing.

> (LUIS BUÑUEL, *My Last Breath*)

Oh valiant hearts, who to your glory came
Through dust of conflict and through battle flame;
Tranquil you lie, your knightly valour proved,
Your memory hallowed in the land you loved.
(JOHN S. ARKWRIGHT, from his hymn, 'The Supreme
Sacrifice')

November 1988. Warm and sunny. On the day before Remembrance Sunday I cycle past the church on Chasse-Marais, a tractor parked, a boy hosing down the Cenotaph.

Sunday is cloudless, the hats taken down from the tops of wardrobes, taken out of plastic bags, will not blow off today, and the memo that 'In the event of inclement weather Remembrance will be inside facing the Memorial Window in the church' can be disregarded.

A stranger in November is horribly conspicuous. I wander in the old cemetery where horses were tethered during the Occupation, among the anchors and angels on the standing stones. Memorials written in French, not simply pre-Occupation but pre-English invasion.

Old Sark of the census, de Carteret, Falle, Mollet, Hamon, Guille, Drillot, Baker, le Feuvre, Wakely, Carrée, Perrée, Vaudin, Vibert, le Masurier. Hamon married to Baker, Baker

married to de Carteret, Hamon espouse de Vaudin, le Feuvre to
Guille, Hamon to Carrée. . . .

None of the older Sarkese have ever spoken to me about roots.
The word is not current on Sark; knowing who you are and where
you came from is taken absolutely for granted. Belonging, 'Even
if you don't you feel you do,' is only spoken of by English
residents.

There is no doubt, no conflict, links are continuous, dusted on
the sideboard, somewhere in the back of that old drawer. People
live as long as you remember them. History – 'Every family is a
different village, they take it in with their mother's milk' – is not
dead.

> Culture has often been loosely defined as behaviour as
> observed through social relations and material artefacts.
> Although these may provide some raw data for a
> construct of culture they are not in themselves the
> constituents of culture. Culture, in a deeper and
> anthropological sense, includes patterns, norms, rules and
> standards which find expression in behaviour, social
> relations and artefacts. . . . The essential core of culture
> consists of tradition, i.e. historically derived and selected
> ideas and especially their attached values.
> (EMANUEL DE KADT, *Tourism: Passport to Development?*)

After a year's work on and off the island I am now considerably
more jittery than the anthropologist was when I met him. I don't
wear stripes any more and am easily unnerved, boat flu leads to
bike dreams.

A flat bicycle tyre on the mainland is a nuisance. On Sark, if
you're feeling hunted, it's nothing short of a mortification. I have
taken to cycling very fast around the little roads with the result
that on a hair-raising spin away from Little Sark I managed to get
two flat tyres at once. I now have a boy's bike and a handlamp for
dark nights which jiggles unconvincingly in the basket. I still
cycle fast to avoid imagined confrontations, but I dream at night
of coming a cropper in more ways than seventeen. My tapes are
all 'Ave Maria', my notebooks make no sense, the book refuses to

arrange itself in any sort of order, in bike-speak the chain falls off and I cannot find the brakes.

This November I am sharing my patch with a Dutch journalist whose article about Sark is loosely based on how the island will fit into the Europe of 1992. He is only here for a week and is quite happy with his two-wheeler. Whilst I skulk in the graveyard he is out there, centre-stage, taking pictures of the Remembrance Day procession.

We gather around the Cenotaph. The robed choir – men, women and children – is most representative of the island's population, indigenous and otherwise. The congregation consists largely of Sark's first and second eleven – the Seigneur, the doctor, distinguished English ex-pats – and the reserve. The choir sings 'Be Still My Soul', hardly a wind to ruffle the flag or the vicar's gown, everything's going smoothly.

'They have their own way of doing things and the first Remembrance Service was very difficult. I was told loosely what they did and said, "I'll fit in." This year I think at last I got it just about right, the coming in and the going out. It's taken me four years to knock it into shape and it's hard getting the information, when the organ will play, etc. There are half a dozen Methodists on the island and I would like us to get together more. I believe in Ecumenism. There used to be one Remembrance Service at our church at 11.00 and another at the Methodist at three in the afternoon. Logically what I'd like to see here is an island church.'

In 1817 the British Government, alarmed by the rapid spread of Methodism in England, where it was regarded in many quarters as a subversive movement, established a fund of £1,000,000 for the building of Anglican Churches in the new industrial centres of population to counteract the influence of the numerous Methodist chapels that had sprung up in these areas. The Seigneur conceived the idea of restoring the status and prestige of the Anglican Church in Sark by obtaining a grant from this fund to build a new Church. . . . When the new Church was completed . . . in 1821, the new Seigneur sought to enlist

86

the support of the Islanders by selling 36 pews in the new
church for sums varying from £5 to £15 to the Tenants of the
Quarantaine; these pews henceforth formed an integral part
of the Tenements, and the money received from the sale of
the pews formed the nucleus of a fund for the maintenance of
the Church.

(*Fief of Sark*)

We know a passer-by who, one Sunday in the lovely
island of Sark heard in the courtyard of a farm this verse
from an old French Huguenot hymn, sung very solemnly
in chorus by religious voices with the low-pitched
intonation of the Calvinists:

> 'Everyone stinks, stinks, stinks,
> Like a decaying carcass.
> There is only, only, only gentle Jesus
> Who has a pleasing smell.'

It is a gloomy, almost painful thought that people died in
the Cevennes with those words on their lips. That verse,
extremely funny without meaning to be, is tragic. People
laugh at it; they should cry instead. At this verse, Bossuet
– one of the forty members of the Academie Française –
shouted: 'Kill! Kill!'

(VICTOR HUGO, *L'Archipel de la Manche*)

'At 8.45 we would go to assembly at the church every morning.
We are Methodists and I can remember when a special preacher
came across it was standing room only.'

Though other services often include a French hymn this one is
conducted entirely in English.

In those days [late nineteenth and early twentieth
century] the Church of England service was conducted
entirely in French, which made it difficult to find a
suitable English parson. The first French clergy that I
remember was a Monsieur Vermeil, who demonstrated
his anti-British feelings by skipping the prayers for Queen
Victoria. On these occasions my father would rise in

wrath from the family pew which was, of course, the front
pew, stamp out of the church and go straight home to write a
letter to the Bishop. The Bishop would protest to Monsieur
Vermeil and for the next few weeks he would unwillingly
read the prayers until he'd skip them again, and again there
was the same angry performance from Father. . . . The
Reverend Louis Napoleon Seichan, who replaced Monsieur
Vermeil, was a law unto himself. If he disliked any
parishioner who had died he would refuse to allow the
Church pall to be used on the coffin. He once went so far as
to take his maidservant to help him pull down a tombstone
that had been erected to a man he hated. In English that was
not good, he used to announce that the Collection would be
for the 'Organist's Fun'.

(DAME OF SARK, *Autobiography*)


The French which the old inhabitants of the islands speak is
perhaps not altogether their fault.

(VICTOR HUGO, *L'Archipel de la Manche*)


The old man speaks Patois on his new digital wall phone, his flow
occasionally interspersed with English, 'Bugger me!' Though
most of the middle-aged Sarkese understand Patois, it is only the
old man's generation who speak it fluently, unconsciously,
without a second thought. The fact that the language is dying is
regretted, the prevailing attitude that it's just another part of the
old life passing, an inevitable event or consequence of Sark as it is
today. If Patois is to be preserved it will be as a museum
language, a collector's item in a glass case, a project undertaken
by an enthusiastic outsider who will probably get it wrong. The
passing of Sark Patois is an example of how the indigenous
population regard poor Juliet. They're so accustomed to her
performance that they no longer take it in, they wait for her to
collapse on stage, but by then it's frequently too late.

'When you had an English husband you had to speak English
because he didn't know our language, you see, then of course –
you speak to the husband, you talk to the children. . . . There are

88

no books in Patois but it's still written though, my cousin she writes it beautifully. I can write a few words as well but I'm not going to tell you they're spelt right or anything. It's just an abbreviation of the good French isn't it? Mind you there are Patois words in Little Sark that are different to ours, not all that many but there are.'

'A man used to come here, he was interested in Patois which amused me because, whatever we said, he wrote it down. You make mistakes in spelling no one can correct them. He had a bigger tape recorder than yours.'

'The Patois he wrote in that book, well I don't understand it. He must have been deaf.'

'I was born in 1906. Patois was the language of the home, my children understand every word but they don't speak it. It's silly, I think, I think they should. You see they could have been laughed at when they first spoke it. Because our parents not knowing English at all sort of spoke pidgin English, it could have been that the children would have been self-conscious. Patois was the language of the playground. Another thing, mind you, a lot of Sark girls . . . a lot of men came, well I think it must have started during the silver mines but anyway . . . lots of different English people came to work and married Sark girls and of course they didn't know the Patois so it was a case of learning English. We knew English because of our teacher Miss Shaw, she was very, very good. My mother knew English as well but not perfect. I think that's why the language has died down.'

The Vicar of Sark is a thoughtful man, not the sherry-swilling, bridge-playing, live wire some of his English parishioners apparently expect. We talk in his study, his dog's Bonio biscuits on a shelf behind me. He is generous with his time and breaks off to chat to me from writing a sermon on the Holy Ghost.

'I came to live in the way the Sarkese live, as in Canada one would try to be for the Canadians. One shouldn't try to make it a little corner of England – it's Sark and it's a place in its own right. I've never been invited for a meal in a Sark house. I say, 'Love your neighbour as yourself,' whatever he is, like your own children. It's the joy of getting closer to people wherever you are and if you're here you can't drop into a car and drive away, you have to stick it out. I am priest in charge rather than vicar of this parish. It would have been easier to be vicar but my bishop told me, 'You are responsible for the care of the souls in your parish.' A lot of them remember the old vicar who still lives on the island. I remember after my first welcoming service one of the "cocktail" set came up to me, "Do you play bridge?"'

The Rev. Seichan, was truly as remarkable a character and a personality as I ever met. He was an ardent supporter of the Bonapartist Party and, like so many of Sark's vicars, was of French extraction. An unusually tall man, about six feet six inches, he was between sixty and seventy years of age when I first met him.

Of extremely attractive appearance, he started life as a Roman Catholic priest, but left that Faith and joined the Established Church of England in order to marry a lady of the Protestant Faith. . . . In his heart of hearts he always remained a Roman Catholic and the services he conducted on Sark were always of an advanced Anglo-Catholic nature. This did not add to his popularity with the Sarkees, who are distinctly Low Church in their sentiments. In consequence, many of them ceased their connection with the Church and joined the Wesleyans.

I never knew what caused the coolness between Mr. Seichan and Mr. Collings [Seigneur, Dame's father], but I have very good reason to believe that it was due to the vicar's interest in local politics and his attempts to influence the islanders to his way of thinking in various local disputes.

Mr. Seichan was somewhat eccentric in his mode of attire. He always appeared with a sort of black cloak of a Bersaglieri pattern, part of which was thrown over his left shoulder, while his hat resembled that worn in Paris before the Franco-Prussian War.

He often dined at my bungalow and was very fond of introducing into the conversation and discussing religious topics, which was not my strong point. I always regarded him as an extremely clever man and wasted on Sark.

(CAPTAIN ERNEST PLATT, *Sark as I found it*)

'It's the scale of the parish that makes it wonderful. I am unable to cycle or drive, you might say Sark and I were made for each other in a way. Each new member contributes something, we all have a cross. In a parish of this nature it is impossible to be off duty. I try and work an eight-hour day. I love to walk but one cannot be off duty even on the beach.'

The vicar disliked the sea so much that his daily walk was only taken along the shady lane leading from the vicarage to one of the hotels. By not walking quite as far as the hotel he could avoid the sight of the sea.

(EVE ORME, *Sark Remembered*)

'I see Sark as a mission outpost, I see myself as a man among men. No the bell doesn't ring for every year of life at Sark funerals, it rings when they get it ringing. The congregation averages fifty over the year, there are about eighty communicants here. What we have here is Churchianity not Christianity. I don't really like to baptise babies without tuition for the parents and I don't think children should be confirmed until they're eighteen or so. Sark doesn't like change at all. I feel that when you're worshipping God in the church words are secondary to heart's desires but I still use the 1662 communion service. The elderly make it to church somehow in the winter and, like in the choir, there is a very good cross-section. I go to the school once a week, there is a lot to do there, church is more than music and biblically-based stories.

'The Church of England is the state church and you feel very much like part of the supply industry but also very much here,

91

you are a close member of the whole family, someone they can approach. It's taken three years, softly, softly, catchee monkey.

'We're closer to the realities here. Life, birth and death, we know what we are and who our grannies slept with. The Sark people understand their history. Death and funerals are more difficult to bear. I am a veteran of 1500 funerals on the mainland and yet I find funerals here very stressful.'

> In cities no one notices specific dying. Dying is a quality
> of the air. It's everywhere and nowhere. Men shout as
> they die, to be noticed, remembered for a second or two.
> To die in an apartment instead of a house can depress the
> soul, I would imagine, for several lives to come. In a town
> there are houses, plants in bay windows. People notice
> dying better. The dead have faces, automobiles. If you
> don't know a name, you know a street name, a dog's
> name. 'He drove an orange Mazda.'
>
> (DON DELILO, *White Noise*)

'The colonial types are not ecumenical but it doesn't matter to me who people are or who they live with. Sark reminds me of my childhood, of holidays when I was a child. The Sark people are superstitious, only need church for baptism, marriage and death. I have confirmed two children since I took over this parish.'

Standing in the sunshine round the Cenotaph the minute's silence connects and disconnects, Hamons, Guilles, Carrées, colonials, Enniskillen, and the sound of a tractor working in the distance.

'In my father's time there was no work on Sunday, these days people have gone mad, I mean, tractors around all day on Sunday?'

> The Methodists did with the English Sunday what they
> did with the English theatre. For the mass of the working
> classes there was only one day on which they were free
> from the discipline of mill and workshop. On that day

they were refused recreation for mind or body, music or games, beauty of art or nature. They sought diversions where they could find them. The Yorkshire and Lancashire papers are full of complaints that the youth of the large towns spend Sunday gambling in the streets, or in drunkenness and brutal sports, and that the behaviour of the populace was distressing and inconvenient to respectable people. An engineer who had been abroad described the difference in this respect between English and Continental life. He told the Factory Commission that at Mulhausen, where most of the people were Protestant, the workmen went to church in the morning and spent the rest of the day in the country playing games, whereas in England 'a man can do nothing but go to a public house on Sunday, and when there you can do nothing but drink.'

(J. L. and BARBARA HAMMOND, *The Bleak Age*)

'Too many people get away with too many things. All the tractors are going out on Sunday now for farm work and even a couple of years ago that would never have been allowed. There are no boats on Sundays and you're not meant to light any bonfires, use any machinery, like chainsaws, trimmers, you're not meant to but people do. It's just slacked off. People get away with a lot of things, once there were these two people who were constables and they even told the Dame that she was breaking the island law.'

A sabbatarian council has failed to prevent Caledonian MacBrayne's new Sunday ferry sailings between Skye and the Outer Hebridean island of North Uist. An application by Western Isles Islands Council for a by-law preventing the ferry company from using the pier at Lochmaddy, North Uist on Sundays, was dismissed as unreasonable.'

(*Independent*, June 1989)

**Sunday Rest**
Sunday is a special day for those who live in Sark
In bed a-sleeping others rising with the lark
Sunday is a quiet day no trips from other lands
The faithful make their way to church and the vicar

reads the bans
The housewife bakes the Sunday roast and father pulls
the weeds
The neighbours call for gossip or doing useful deeds
Sunday is a rest day for doing as you please
The carriage horses crop the grass and the drivers take
their ease
But what I like most about Sunday I don't mind telling
you
Is that Sunday is the one day when I've got no work to
do.
(THOMAS LONG, extract from TV documentary, *The
Highway*)

Sunday rules by custom, which is far more despotic than
law. This King of England that is Sunday has Melancholy
for his Prince of Wales. Boredom is his by right . . . . An
unfortunate French woman inn-keeper in Guernsey served
a glass of beer to a sight-seer; as it was Sunday she got
two weeks in prison. A refugee, a shoemaker, wants to
work on Sundays to feed his wife and children; he closes
his shutters so that people will not hear him hammering;
if they do he will be fined; one Sunday, an artist who has
just arrived from Paris stopped by the roadside to sketch a
tree; a centenier went up to him and called on him to stop
this scandalous behaviour.
(VICTOR HUGO, *L'Archipel de la Manche*)

'On Saturday nights a whole set of clean clothes was laid out for
Sunday. Sundays was far stricter. Years ago when there was a
funeral no one would have dreamt of driving a tractor or
anything. If there was a funeral all the curtains were drawn along
the route, I remember that. We had to go to Sunday School, had
to go to church. We weren't allowed to knit or sew a button on,
not even have the wireless on. In our house we could knit but not
at granny's, we wouldn't have done it at granny's out of respect.
On Saturday we cleaned our shoes for Sunday and learnt what we
had to learn for Sunday School, word perfect, and peel the
vegetables for the next day. As you undressed on Saturday night

your clothes were put for Monday's washing. There was so much discipline.'

After the service the Dutch journalist hurries off, the British Legion disperse, the choir disrobes, the first eleven, asking one or another home for drinks, cycle gamely off.

I stay for a while among the Hamons and Guilles, churchyards being as good a place as any to try to sort things out.

The news that I am writing about Sark is only greeted with enthusiasm when the word is misheard as 'Sartre'. In this instance the sentences I have come to use to follow the revelation as defence/attack – 'I imagine you think it's terribly dull' – compounds the confusion. When 'Sark' is finally established as the subject the reaction is, from those who know it, simply, 'Oh,' from those who don't, 'Where's that?' On Sark the situation is reversed. The Sarkese aren't up on Sartre but Sark – it's the centre of the universe, quite obvious, almost admirable, that it and I should want to get to grips.

In bleak moments, 'People are so much the same, is anyone more interesting here than anywhere else?' At low tide, 'She went dotty over that book didn't she?' I wonder.

> If we wish to know about a man we ask, 'What is his story' for each of us is a biography, a singular narrative constructed continually, unconsciously, by, through and in us, through our perceptions, feelings, thoughts, actions and not least our discourse. Biologically, physiologically we are not so different from each other, historically as narratives – we are each of us unique.
> (OLIVER SACKS, *The Man who Mistook his Wife for a Hat*)

> The seaman tells stories of winds, the ploughman of bulls; the soldier details his wounds, the shepherd his sheep.
> (PROPERTIUS)

The Sarkese talk of the farming, the tourists, the Occupation, the Patois, the way things used to be. Can these particulars mean anything to us? Do we simply add them to our fund of information or can stories, as I believe they can, perform some peculiar miracle of osmosis? If novelists, as Doris Lessing claims, 'write their way into becoming more human', then readers and listeners should be allowed to get in on the act. At low tide it is this idea that keeps me going. The Sarkese tell their stories and their stories become our clothes. Their stories add another layer of understanding and of warmth, they help in some incidental, happy way to keep out the chill of what it is to be a human being.

Sark is not a dramatic story – yet. Unlike St Kilda – that image of the islanders standing dry-eyed on the boat that evacuated them, watching their island until it disappeared beyond the horizon – it has neither committed suicide nor been done to death. But Sark in its present state is closer to us all than Sartre. Juliet, like Kavanagh's peasant, like a plant at the back of the flower bed, is dying of old age:

> He circles around and around wondering why it
>     should be.
> No crash,
> No drama.
> That was how his life happened.
> No mad hooves galloping in the sky,
> But the weak, washy way of true tragedy –
> A sick horse nosing around the meadow for a clean
>     place to die.
>             (PATRICK KAVANAGH, *The Great Hunger*)

When St Kilda was evacuated in 1930 many of the islanders were glad to go: 'support for the evacuation had come from the other young men on the island who . . . were weary of the hard life on Hirta.' The essential problem on St Kilda was that it was too far away; the problem on Sark is quite the opposite.

The semi-isolation of the island which protected it from plague in the sixteenth century is the very isolation that has made it attractive to outsiders in the twentieth; its strength has become its weakness. Tourism has accelerated changes that would have happened anyway, and few of the indigenous population would really leap at the chance to swap the combine harvester for the sickle or the bucket for the tap. The twentieth century, with its electricity, television, tourism, has sunk its teeth into Sark and is shaking it like a rat. In such a situation it is some comfort to point the finger, lay the blame. Though the twentieth century is at the back of everything, it is the English residents, a symptom, not a cause, who get it in the neck. It is the change in the make-up of the population which has created among the older generation a profound sense of loss. Some – 'I never wanted to walk out with a Sark girl' – always found their partners beyond Sark but none seem to have been prepared for the flood of English residents who have made the place their own, who, however well intentioned, have changed the nature of the island life.

'Dwindling' is the word that echoes round this graveyard, cultural drift, ebb tide. The past here is not simply a convenient stick with which to beat the present but rather a faint music the ear strains for when yet another incident, individual, confirms what, in bits and pieces, dribs and drabs, is now irrevocably lost.

> So there I sat, listening and watching. The Ride gradually
> drifted away. It clung pitifully to either side of the road,
> letting the constant stream of cars and motorcycles pass.
> A bunch of people were trailing behind. A pathetically
> small bunch. Fewer people come to the Ride every
> year. . . . Yes even after the war it was still worth
> something. We thought that we could build a completely
> new world. That people would return to folk ways. That
> the Ride of the Kings would once again gush forth from
> the depths of their lives. We wanted to help it all to
> happen. We organized one folk festival after the next. But
> a fountainhead can't be organized. And if it doesn't gush,
> it doesn't exist. Look how we have to squeeze out our
> songs, our Rides, everything. They're the last drops, the
> very last drops.
>
> (MILAN KUNDERA, *The Joke*)

# 7

# Pieces of Silver

In the sixteenth century Helier de Carteret apportioned his island into forty tenements or holdings. The owners of these holdings, the quarantine tenants, each had a seat in the island parliament, Chief Pleas. In the twentieth century many of the tenement holders sold their holdings and forfeited their birth-rights as a result.

'The tenements were sold and not stolen, there was no fraud. What I am dead against is people that say, oh well, what are they moaning about, they sold their heritage, it's their fault. But many years ago Sark was very, very poor. I mean if a man earned a pound a week he was lucky. He'd earn about six shillings if he had his midday meal, that sort of thing, they were really poor and that's why they were fisherman/farmers, so as to have their own milk and butter, a good diet.

'Supposing you had a tenement and there's no living, you can't see a living with a wife and family here, so you move over to Guernsey. You've got a tenement but you've got no money so you have to go all the way to Guernsey. A rich man is over here, offers you a vast sum of money in your eyes in those days which is going to take you over the other side and have a little nest egg. What are you going to do?

'It started after the 1914–18 war. They could have refused the offer but then they'd have been poor for the rest of their days.'

Currently there is a remarkably wide choice of Sark property on the market, including the tenement Clos de la Ville with a bungalow and two chalets, offered by several agents . . . for £350,000. It includes nearly 20 vergees (just under 8 acres). Also on the market . . . is Sark's excellent Stocks Hotel with accommodation for 46 plus staff and family rooms. It has a fine swimming pool and peaceful gardens. The price guide is £430,000. Other Sark properties available include one or two small chalets and a beautiful stone-built long house called L'Ecluse, next door to Le Seigneurie (the Seigneur's residence); it has four self-catering holiday units, but the price of £175,000 buys only a 35-year lease. A freehold house, called Maison Pommier, with superb gardens is available for £300,000.

(*Daily Telegraph*, June 1988)

'My mother married a farmer at the turn of the century. His people had left the tenement in a derelict condition so it meant that the place was falling down. Well, my mother kept visitors for years and in the winter that money that she earned in the summer – it had a thatched roof – it either went to patch up the roof or mend the gable end or put a new door . . . there was always, always something, so they were never better off. The money they earned went back and then summer came, something happened . . . weren't they better off if they really wanted to go away? What's the good of clinging to something that's going to keep you miserable for the rest of your days? You know, if only people had known what was going to happen and that money was going to be so plentiful as it is now, they would have clung to their heritages I'm sure.'

Just a few weeks ago, a 100-acre estate was put up for sale on Sark. With this went a seat in the local parliament, a twelve-roomed granite cottage and a silver mine which hasn't been worked for very many years.

(*Radio Trek*, 1946)

'I'll tell you about the sale of tenements,' confides a middle-aged Sarkee. 'A lot were sold to outsiders from spite, the quarrelling among the families.'

By the late 1950s less than half of the forty tenements were still owned by Sark families. . . . As the value of property began to rise to a level way beyond the average Sark pocket, it was inevitably Sibyl who was made the scapegoat for allowing such a situation to develop and there was a strong feeling in some quarters that she cared more about getting her 'treizième' of the purchase price of the tenements, than about the calibre of the new owners. But once an islander had made up his mind to sell his property, there was little she could do to stop him, providing the purchaser qualified under the terms of the old charter. There is evidence too, although not generally known, of her trying to dissuade some Sarkese from leaving their farms and reducing or even waiving her 'treizième' to those who wished to buy tenements. She also refused to give her congé to certain would-be buyers, whom she considered would be unsuitable residents.

(BARBARA STONEY, *Sibyl, Dame of Sark*)

'In the early fifties we were worried about the balance between Sark and English but it hasn't really got worse because these farms or properties being bought by the English, the prices are so high now that the locals can't touch them. If any tenement has been sold recently they were already in English hands and are being sold again to someone else. If it is already sold to an Englishman no Sarkee can retraite if he sells again. If it is a Sark person it can be retraited until the seventh generation. Once it's changed hands from Sarkee to Englishman you've had your chips.'

'We had six weeks to retrait. I can assure you it was a worrying time.
'It all happened one evening, we were bundling wheat in the field. I kept telling my wife that I wanted it and by the time we came back we discussed it and the following morning I went to the Greffe Office to find out how long and that. I had three days left to do it and I didn't have the money. I couldn't get to Guernsey in time. We were great friends, the bank manager and

myself – and you're dealing with a local lad, and in fact, we were related – and I went to see him and he advised me what to do. He said your father's got a bank account at the bank, you go and ask him to ring up the bank manager in Guernsey, if he'll make you a cheque for what you need for your farm which will cover it until you've got a chance to go over to Guernsey and make arrangements. 1946, I hardly slept for a week. I said to the wife, there's always one thing, if we see that we can't do it we can always sell it again. When we told my father about it he said, "If you intend buying it to farm it then buy it, but if you want to buy it and then sell it for a few years time then leave it where it is."'

By 1967, following an invasion by wealthy outsiders wanting to share the tax advantages and the tranquillity, only 93 of the 236 dwellings on the island were occupied by Sarkese. This trend, happily, has been reversed, but there are still opportunities for property purchase by outsiders.

(*Daily Telegraph*, June 1988)

'To me, from the day I went there to the day I came back I felt it was a terrific privilege to have lived on Sark. I've lived in other villages, I live here, but I still regard this village as the villagers' village and not mine. You can't go and take over in small, rural communities to my mind, not if you're going to be happy with them.'

'Some people came to live on the island and they rubbed the Sark people up the wrong way because they treated the Sark people like peasants, quite nice people but they had done colonial service and had been used to their little black slaves, they regarded themselves as important. And I remember two Sark people came into the shop one day, and they said, "These people, they've got to learn we're not their peasants," and I don't blame them.'

'I remember the feeling of freedom on Sark in the forties and the sense of cliques. The population then was about 390 indigenous, 275 other and remained so until it took off in the fifties.'

(SEBASTIAN PEAKE)

'We're overpopulated in this island. They say our people have to have a place to live, but the unfortunate part, it isn't the locals that are living in those places, they are others.

'I don't mind the tourists – this summer I'm taking my little grandchild who's only two up to deliver the milk in the morning – "Ah. Please hang on a minute," if I was stopped 200 times to have my photograph taken, but it gives those tourists pleasure. It's the same when they ask directions, they've taken the trouble to come to the island and the least you can do is show them as much as you can.

'What really gets up my nose is when the English people come over here and buy a property. They put a bloomin' notice up, "Private". If we'd put "Private" up the top of Harbour Hill no one would be here anyway. You'd never see a "Private" board on any of our Sark homes. They've been coming on holiday for years and years, they've been walking all our fields and we've shown them as much as we can. They come, buy a plot of land, they rent a house, they're not here five minutes and it's "Private", that is upsetting. We've not been used to it, we've always been used to making everybody welcome. They can walk where they like, they treat us with respect, we don't mind.'

The ordinance relating to trespass in Sark is rather elastic, and it is almost impossible to succeed in an action.

In a test case which was heard soon after I took up my residence on the island an English resident brought an action for trespass against a Sarkee. He did not succeed but made himself extremely unpopular with the islanders until his position became unbearable and he had to quit Sark.

(CAPTAIN ERNEST PLATT, *Sark as I found it*)

The other thing which I think worth noting is people's awareness of their 'Sarkness'. The vast majority of English people feel that the majority of the inhabitants are English. The majority of Sark people believe that the majority are Sark. In fact the majority (by about 100) were not born on the Channel Islands. Regardless of the actual state of things, if you believe an opinion it may as well be a fact and, in an anthropological sense, the opinion is much more important than the fact.

(RICHARD PELERINE, anthropologist working on Sark 1988, interview with *Guernsey Evening Press*)

'I think we now feel that Sark has gone, it's not Sark any more. Once upon a time there were forty tenements as you know, well, once upon a time the English crept in, crept in, but we always said, "Ah well, there's only 16 of them" because it would have been twenty you see, half way. But, it's gradually crept up now that there's more of them as tenants than Sark people, we feel that Sark isn't Sark any more.'

# 8

## *Robinson Crusoe*

Anyone who has seen the Channel Islands loves them; anyone who has lived there has a high opinion of them.

A noble race, small but with a big heart, lives there. Their soul is from the sea. These Channel Islanders are a race apart. They consider themselves superior somehow to people from the mainland and they are arrogant with the English, who in turn sometimes refer disdainfully to 'these three or four vases of flowers in an ornamental lake'.

(VICTOR HUGO, *L'Archipel de la Manche*)

The Sarkees in general are very secretive. They have acquired the art of carefully guarding their innermost thoughts. Though polite to the extreme in their manner, I have, however, come to the conclusion after a long experience, that it is impossible to break down the barrier which exists between the Sarkees and the English, whether the latter be residents or visitors.

(CAPTAIN ERNEST PLATT, *Sark as I found it*)

'I got invalided out of the navy in 1935, they gave me two years to live. I was in a pretty bad way when I come out, eyesight and double pneumonia. I don't think they had penicillin then, I was in Portland hospital for a long time, my father, they sent for him, he came up, he was there a couple of days before I knew he was there. There wasn't a pension, you had to do so many years before you got that. Oh terrible, my heart was broken, I didn't know what to do, I couldn't work, I was on the dole, what was it? Five and six a week. I gradually began to pick up, I had to walk with two sticks and I had glasses. They got me a job through the naval people. You get sent to the office and you don't know whether it's getting told off or . . . he said, "I want you to go to Sark," and I said, "Where the hell's Sark?"

'The islanders are a bit like the Cornish, more so when I came here. They were so friendly. Three of us palled up together, when we came here first we didn't know anyone, we were working on building La Maseline harbour. In the evenings we used to walk round up near La Ville Roussel, there was a row of cottages and, "Oh come in, have a cup of tea." Christmas there were two or three of us working on the crusher and I went up to the chemist one day and there was a girl came out. I said good morning to her and she said, "Morning" well that was all. That was all and I didn't see her any more until Whit Monday 1939. I happened to go down the Creux harbour to see the visitors coming off the boat, because we used to go down there to see it sometimes, and she was sitting on a bollard and she looked round. "Oh hello," she said, "I haven't seen you for a long time, last time I saw you it was at the chemist shop". So from there it went on.

'She lived with her parents, born in that house over there. I made this garden. I used to be up here a lot before we were married. Maseline Harbour was open in '48 and we were married in '42. In Guernsey for five years during the Occupation.

'After the war there was plenty of jobs to do but I wanted to go away. I wanted to go away for ten years but she wouldn't have it. She said, "You go if you like." I said, "Don't be silly." My elder daughter was born, we was very good because when we was married in 1942 my mother-in-law says, "No family till after the war," so my first daughter was born in 1946. I was born in 1906, she was born in '46 and my younger daughter in '56.

'I used to help on the farm and odd jobs round here. It was a bit difficult to be accepted into a Sark family. I used to get sometimes, you know, "You Englishmen, you don't understand." I was very patient because of my wife you see. I was very tolerant, I still am.

'I stayed a Cornishman, even the lingo. There were some people passed me one day and I heard them say, "Proper job," and I said, "Coo. Good old Cornwall!" My name was "Janner" in the navy. If I go back there, to Cornwall, I go right back into it.

My wife used to laugh but she used to pick up some of it. My wife was descended from the de Carteret clan.'

Few Crusoes have the chance to join a clan. It is the minority who marry into Sark, the majority who come as couples to retire. Sark's English residents, lumped together, blamed for this or that, do not, on close inspection, fit neatly into any of the pigeon holes they're put in. Some come to work on Sark for the season and drift their way to staying on. Others, linked by telephone, fax and computer, drawn by the island's tax-free status, come to work. Some who have bought up tenements create further ill-feeling as absentees, who contribute nothing to the island and live to all intents and purposes elsewhere. Others – and you can't win on an island – enter into island life, know and use the power of their votes, and are considered to be interfering. Most live in bungalows or shacks, in flats created from larger houses. At this end of the century Sark's English population are not just the muslin over the sandwiches, gin and It., ex-pats. The passing of the stereotypic Brit, if in fact it ever existed, is, in the way of Sark, regretted. Yesterday was always better.

'There's quite a few degrees on Sark. We've lost a lot of the colonials, a lot of the gentry. I do think the people who come to Sark now aren't . . . when we were children, that's what I remember most of all, the gentry that came to live on Sark. The people who bought properties on Sark, I was a child, I used to look up to them. Now we have a certain amount of the nouveau riche who don't actually have a lot of the lovely manners and the ways that these other people had, more eccentric, more interesting, there was something special about them, they were wonderful.'

'Poor Brits, they come in and three years later they're telling Sark what to do with their island. I can't stand it. The type who came and stayed on are fine, who lived here since 1948. They're part of Sark and Sark would do anything for them.'

*

The Crusoes form an infinitely varied group who have little else than English nationality in common. Whoever they are, how many there are, where they live and how they do or do not contribute to the island is, as the anthropologist recognised, actually immaterial. The English exist in the mind of the beholder. How people perceive them is what matters, with the result that however they behave as individuals, to the Sarkese they are branded together as a group. How large this group is, how threatening or enhancing, depends who you're talking to and why and when. Facts again are shoved to the periphery, opinion, as ever, is all.

For some Sark equals freedom: 'There's no class, no desirable residential area, no status symbols, no status attached to jobs, no superiority. We're all equals. It's freedom, whatever you did before, and now you're carting, serving behind a bar. . . .'

Others suffer feelings of persecution born of isolation and loneliness which, to complicate the picture even further, depend on the angle the observer chooses to adopt. The flip side of community is the sanctions it imposes, its manner of creating outcasts in its happy wake. Alternatively victimisation may be seen to exist only in the mind of the woman who's frightened of a puncture, of the man who claims the carter tipped a pile of logs onto his dahlia bed on purpose, on the couple who say their lives were made unbearable by tongues wagging behind closed doors.

Crusoe's relationship with his island is rather like a marriage. Some fall for Sark then spend the rest of their lives trying to change her, others fight for a while then grow indifferent. Some who wished to change her admit to becoming as reactionary and conservative as the rest of them after the first ten years. And some – it must be their second marriage – tell you once too often that they are really terribly, terribly happy.

'I had been frequently to holiday on Guernsey before I came to live on Sark and I loved the Channel Islands anyway. I used to finish my two weeks' holiday and go back to catch the plane and there would be this sinking feeling, when you saw this lovely bright clean sky and you thought about going back to the smog.

When I lived in London I never went out without nylons, perfect make-up, carefully chosen clothes. Now I'm wearing a track-suit bottom and an old top, I mean, who cares? When I go back to London one of the first things they say to me is, "Don't you look brown?" and they're so white. The second thing they say is, 'It's high time you went out and bought some new clothes.' I go to Marks and Spencers and I think they're very good; here, Marks and Sparks is the height of elegance. Very, very occasionally I think, Oh it would be nice to get into an evening dress. When I first came here people were still wearing long evening dresses in the evenings and we used to really dress up but it's got more casual at the moment. I expect it will swing back the other way again.

'One of the things that's difficult is, you suddenly think you're totally out of touch. There is no way of telling whether your ideas are a load of rubbish, no feedback. When I lived in London I used to miss desperately the opportunity to go and walk in the country and I missed that far more than I miss now, here, the things that I can't do here. I used to go and stay with people for weekends and revel in the country air and walk. Here, at sunset time if I feel like it I can put all my books on the shelf, go over to Port du Moulin and watch the most spectacular sunset, which is beautiful. I've been doing things here I wanted to do all my life, photography, star gazing . . . I do tapestry, there are so many things to do you just run out of time to do them all. The people who don't survive are those who aren't prepared to tackle anything and who didn't have an enormous range of interests before they came.'

'My sister came here, she worked in hotels, she said, "I've got a job for you, washing pots." That was 1983. I worked in a hotel, I was chamber-maiding. I would start at seven in the morning, make the beds, the season ended in October. I kept coming back, I liked the island. Then I was waitressing, just another face in the crowd, girls like me come and go every year. Then I really thought I could spend a few years here. I couldn't think of anything better so I decided to stay.

'I was really lucky. I got a cottage and no trouble finding work, cleaning jobs and things, working in the Mermaid in the winter, picking children up from school and that. I was quite content in the winter, I really was. I don't have the concentration to watch television, I just read usually. I read a bit on Sark which I've forgotten all about. I've got friends as well. I used to go round for dinner and things like that, I didn't do much. On good days I used to walk, get up early. I used to go to the Eperquerie on Sundays because it used to be quite a distance from where I was, so I used to go up there. I didn't go to Guernsey, I had money left from the summer in the winter so I always had the choice of going. I feel a bit more isolated now because I haven't got the money to go. There was nothing exciting happening or anything like that, I was quite content. I never really thought about going to Guernsey, I don't particularly like Guernsey apart from the shopping that you can't get over here. Clothes are out really, it doesn't matter about clothes over here anyway so I don't feel like I've got to get to the boutiques and see what the latest fashions are. I read the paper, they say, "Why buy the paper, it's the same every day?"

'Some days you don't see anybody, if you want to see people you have to visit. In the summer it's obviously completely different because you're going about more. It used to bother me more when I first came, you see the same old faces. My social life was different then, I used to live in the pub, know what I mean, I used to go for walks but I didn't appreciate the island. Now I get a lot of pleasure out of the island itself, Port du Moulin, the Eperquerie, down at the landing, are my favourite places. I really wanted my parents to come over at one stage to show them, to share it. I found it okay on my own, but when you do mingle with people in the summer you find it hard to settle down again, in the winter I was always on my own.'

You don't need eyesight, you don't need ears. Sark is one big eye, and another big ear.

(MERVYN PEAKE, *Mr. Pye*)

'I used to hear the gossip about a week after, because sometimes I didn't go out and obviously it thrives on gossip here. I mean the things I hear about myself, that gets me down really, things people say just brings you down because they've nothing better to do. People get bored with their lives so they invent. You can't talk to somebody without them thinking you're having an affair with them. I would have thought that's an exaggeration but not after what I've found out recently, gossip. . . .

'People like to see you, what they think you are rather than what you actually are. It's like, I'm a young girl over here, "What the hell does she want over here? She must be up to something or hiding something?" The boring truth is that I go to work and spend a lot of time on my own or with my friends, that's it.

'I think any small community is much the same anyway, be it a village or an island. There's the business about buying the paper as well. You're in the shop buying a paper, on and off I read the *Guardian* mainly. "What do you read the *Guardian* for?" You know, it's sort of . . . you have to explain yourself all the time.

'It's just another place to live, it's a very pretty place, it's a lot better than a lot of other places, but reading the *Guardian* and living here, it's a cop-out, isn't it? . . . . I do get cheesed off with it, I'm like the token liberal and at any dinner party or barbecue, if anyone says anything, I've got to support myself. I'm in the minority all the time, everyone's just conforming. It's easier to conform, I've conformed to live here. I'm sick of all the rages I used to go into, people saying "nigger" or something like that, feminists are a big joke, I don't do it any more. I don't even bother, I just keep my mouth shut, conforming because its easier.'

'There are people I've never spoken to on the island, there are people I would not like to talk to simply because of what I've heard.'

'You can be adopted, you can be a Sarkee within 48 hours if you play your cards right. We're not a greedy race, we ask of everybody that comes to Sark, courtesy. What we object to so much is people coming here because they love it so much and they're not here five minutes before they want to start changing things around. Now that does get under our skin. I mean, why do they want to come here if they want to change it?

'You can always tell. The first week they're here, you can say, "He'll not be here by Christmas. He'll last five years then he'll be gone." Because they're head-over-heels about the island, "What a lovely place", this, that and the other, "We're so grateful to be on Sark". But if you are, "Good morning, lovely morning", this that and the other and not be over the moon, just take things as it is one day and then the other, they're the ones that have got two feet on the ground about Sark.'

'Sark is a cushion, it cushions you. You don't know how to face things any more, even going to Guernsey it's hard to readjust.'

'My father said, "You mustn't waste your time here in this backwater," but really, what more challenging thing could there be, if you can put something into the island? Over here there's no such thing as the country and the city, we're surrounded by friends and in the middle of the action. I like to go to England once a year to restore our sanity, fortunately when we go we manage to convince ourselves that England's horrible. For instance the village where we stayed a woman was murdered when we were staying there and that I found terrifying, police blocking the roads and searching the fields. I'd never dream of going out in the dark in England. We're lucky as a couple because we see a lot of each other. I think you'd be hard put to find a better place to live.'

'The day tripper, then the week or fortnightly person who stays on the island, and then there's the life tripper but he's a tripper just the same. The retired person, he's gone there to get what he can out of Sark. He doesn't like it when you tell him that. The retired person, now, a few of them actually give quite a bit back, it's in their nature, in all sorts of ways they are thoughtful, concerned, intelligent people with their skills they bring with them from the outside world, organising ability and so on. And some of those people have given a lot, but, most of them who go and live there, they want cheap booze and servants and no tax and they're going to grab everything they can and in my view they're as bad as any tripper you can imagine.'

'I was absolutely determined, I would not stay there until my old age, that I would come away however hard it was while I was able to come away and before I had become, in any shape or form, a responsibility to the local people. There was no nurse on the island at that time, no facilities whatever, no nursing home. If you were ill enough to be in hospital the St John's ambulance, Flying Christine boat came across. If it was too rough for that the lifeboat came across and fetched you and that was it. I believe it is the same now. Beyond that you were dependent on the good nature of the Sark people, and they were good-natured in those days, and I saw others, elderly ladies on their own, who didn't attempt to move and the Sark ladies simply nursed them and cared for them and looked after them to their death. I thought that wasn't on, they had more than enough to cope with with their own people. When I lived there there were no funds or pensions to help or anything and the Sark people are marvellous like that, they would look after anybody. I vowed I would not let that happen.'

'Every family is a different village, family businesses. . . . Deep down in their hearts they prefer it to be a Sark person working and you know what you can do or you can't do, so it goes on. . . . Here, married for 3,000 years and you're still an outsider. When you get older you see all these things, and when I was younger, wilder, I didn't. I find it's a very closed community when you look into it. When you come from different cultures and you do things a different way and sometimes they say things to you. I came from Ireland, I had to be strong, they can make you very upset. If they don't like you they'll keep onto you and their words will hurt you so much they'll push you off and you can't take any more. I think if they like you they'll take your part, doesn't matter how serious it is. I would never give in and in the end they saw me so strong in mind and body they just left me alone. But the first person in Sark I ever answered back, he was an old man from Little Sark, I remember that. As I got older and steadier . . . what I thought years ago are two different minds. I think you have to live your life but a certain lot of people are going to spoil it here because it's like the Falklands and they win it for their children, their jealousy, their greed. You've always got to think in the back of your mind that Sark is Sark, the people have a kind of togetherness.'

'There's the First Eleven: Seigneur, doctor, Seneschal, very wealthy English residents, elderly English retired, the bank manager, Midland, not Nat West. The Second Eleven is mainly British retired, and the reserves are people of local standing, some Sark people, not just trade. The lines get blurred, of course, but there's not much rising through the ranks.'

'Sark men don't like it if you talk too much. This is still a male-orientated society and I do miss the sort of society where everyone piles in around the dinner table and talks. I find it a bit limiting and in all fairness a great many of them haven't been educated to expect anything more than family life and bringing up children and they aren't extremely interested in things. The attitude to women . . . men here still think as men used to think in England fifty years ago. Not just Sark men, it rubs off on all the other men, given half the chance they revert and they are given half the chance! The women do sit on Chief Pleas if they are tenement holders but there are still women who never even attend Chief Pleas because they consider it to be far above their heads and whether anything would drag them into court to speak up I don't know. The younger generation are almost as reticent as the older ones and some of the old men are living virtually in a different century.'

'The keen English community . . . you're frowned upon if you over-step the mark. "Guernsey yobs", you know, "Sark's idyllic. You don't come over here to drink, you come to drink in the beauty. It reflects badly on the island . . ." People do drink too much over here. It's a known fact they've got nothing else to do. It's good to be good, do things for the community, be seen to be involved in local affairs, that sort of thing.'

'I came, the summer ended, the winter season started and all the societies started up. I went immediately to the thing I loved best of all which was the theatre group and joined that. "Are you prepared to go on stage?" they said, well, keep me off! I'd been in such a group in Hampstead before, places where you're allowed to be third wardrobe mistress if you were lucky. The first play we did was '1066 And All That' and I was cast as a fairy and at that stage I was fifteen and a half stone. I was enormous and I came on as the fairy and went *en point* for about two seconds and if you'll make a fool of yourself you're immediately accepted in the theatre group, you see. At the play party I was asked if I wanted to learn to drive a horse and carriage. Because I had to do the tourism bit round the island – and in those days we did much longer tours – I dived into the history and found out an awful lot about Sark that I would have got through slowly otherwise so I could tell my passengers about what we were going past. It was the drought summer, we all had all sorts of problems about watering the horses and keeping the carriages going. Because I drove a carriage I was accepted into the working population and that's the important part.'

'If you want to you stay badly enough you'll make it work. I mean, I worried, I really worried and yet it was so easy. It was quite a daunting prospect at one time, I thought I would miss things, I really did. I've done what I wanted to do, I've had my own home, I've had a proper working life like most people, nine to five and evenings off and weekends. The beauty of the island gave me peace and still does, sketching and writing, but you get lazier and lazier, you can do less and less.'

'Every solution here is to get off if things get you down. When things go wrong for you or get you down they say "For God's sake get yourself off here before it's too late, before it gets a hold of you." Every solution is to get off and it's very hard to take it when the people have been here for fifteen years or more and they're telling you to leave because they don't think it's doing you any good. It's just another place to live. I like to know what's going on in local politics but I'm not a tenement holder or never will be so it doesn't involve me. If friends left I might go, I'd like to get off for a break.'

'People aren't remembered after they've gone. You can actually leave the place and come back and no one realises you've gone. It's very strange, you talk to people about someone who was here a few years ago, they just forget, carry on living now, forget about the people who've gone. They don't remember people because they get used to saying goodbye, it's just a natural progression of people through, back, "How long are you here for this time?" and then off they go again.

'My opinion is that everyone here is here because they've got a little bit of fame. Everybody knows them, that's why actors enjoy it here, because you're known. Everyone has their own little bit of fame here rather than somewhere else where you'd have to do something incredibly outstanding. You can make your name here. I know the son of an actor and his father said, "What's he doing over there?" He's well known over here, we all like to show off.'

'I think you're aware of what other people may think of you. You mustn't sit in the pub and complain that it's dull, you have to go out and find people who are interesting to you, a good bunch of friends who have similar stimulating conversations! Pretty awful without a girlfriend. I used to live on Little Sark when I first came here, on my own. Getting up and talking to someone is quite important. I'm always wondering whether I'm doing the right thing in life and whether I would be wondering the same thing in England, I hope I would. There is a sense of missing out but when I was in England I thought I'd love to come back here. It certainly had a bit of a pull on me. Wherever I worked abroad I wanted to come back.'

\*

'I want this idea to shine in my head. I'd like to do something. I'd like some brilliant idea to hit me in the face one day and I'll pack up and go. No major dramas apart from what I've created for myself, I'll just run out of steam one day and I'll think, "oh" and just go.'

# 9

# *School*

'People say we ought to spend more on education, that children should stay on after fifteen. We don't need more education for living here.'

'If I'd known I was going to live so long I might have done all sorts of things. . . .'

Talking to the older generation of Sarkese who went to school in and around the 1920s, marked differences in attitudes to education appear between the women and the men. Whilst to both education appears to have been at times irregular and haphazard, the women seem to set more store by education for its own sake. School is often remembered, particularly by the men, for the values it instilled, the strictness of the teachers, rather than for 'book learning' which was regarded, and to an extent still is, as incidental, and if not irrelevant then cosmetic.

'I started off my schooling days down at the school but then it broke up and they had to repair it and it was closed for nearly a twelve month. At that time there was a school teacher who used to take pupils and the parents had to pay and when my mother wanted me to go she could only take me in the evenings. I used to go at six o'clock and I must have been about seven or eight and it was the case that I was working all day on the farm and that. I didn't learn much, I've learnt more since. I went on till about fourteen but I couldn't, you know, study. I've never been a bad boy ever, I was no better than anybody else, I was on my own with the teacher, I felt very tired at times although it was a very,

very good teacher. I was the eldest boy and my sister's two years older than I am and it was the case that I had to do quite a lot of work. I was milking the cows at the age of six and seven and as soon as I could handle a cow I was on to driving horses and what have you, I was forced to do it.'

'My mum and dad had been very good at school, always, and they helped you with your homework. We played hockey and tennis, we were only girls, not mixed, girls between five and fourteen and the boys, fourteen of them the same. We had slates and bead-framed abacus and a blackboard with an easel. We learnt four languages. Patois was the language of home and we had English, French and German and we learnt shorthand typing, book-keeping and music.'

'I went to school in the afternoon, my husband went in the evenings. I have still got some of my exercise books from when I was at school. We learnt sewing, no knitting. My mother used to knit a lot, stockings or jerseys. I learnt plain sewing at school, chemises.'

'Sark had the same school teacher for fifty, sixty years and he taught us respect. If we hadn't respected the Seigneur, well. . . . He was very strict. When I was fourteen and two months I went to work for a retired school master from Mauritius. I earned 11 shillings at first then 22 shilings. When I got married in 1939 he upped it to a proper man's wage of 24 shillings. I remember the first morning I went to work my father asked my mother how much he should ask for me, eight or ten shillings. She suggested ten shillings but he still wasn't sure. When my father got out of the house he still wasn't sure, "Oh I don't know," he said.
    '"Is that the boy?"
    '"Yes."
    '"How much do you want for the boy?"
    '"Ten shillings."
    'He used to repair clocks during the day, one day I remember I went to the horse show with another boy then came back to feed

the chickens. The man was cross, he took two shillings off. "How long for?" I asked. "At my own discretion," he said. He took two shillings off my pay for six weeks. Still, on these small wages I managed to save £22. In 1936, the year that King George IV died, I bought a radio. January 10th, a portable on the never-never. I was very worried about it. I remember coming home, I'd been courting, I was living in the Avenue then, and the radio said, "No further news," at 11.30 p.m., then at five to twelve, "The King's life is coming to a close." '

'I went to school at the Manoir, the girls' school. We started at five years old but then the Seneschal [the magistrate] had a row with our wonderful school teacher and she left. Then we kept on having different school teachers, three or four different ones. We were always starting again, it spoilt our education. Then Miss Shaw opened the private school, my old teacher and she taught my children and my grandchildren. She had a brother in England and before or after the occupation she went and looked after him. We were taught in English and we had the vicar every Friday morning to teach us French.'

'Have a look through the school windows, remind you of your early days? Children here leave at fifteen but they can take the Eleven Plus and go to Guernsey if they pass, boarding. They're quite up to date, they've got everything, televisions . . . not computers no.'

The junior school is next door to the prison, diminutive two-wheelers propped against its walls. There's a mini bike rush-hour before nine and after three, and in the winter, when the Avenue is almost deserted, the calls and shouts of the children in the playground can be heard down at the Colinette, up by the church.

The senior school on Chasse Marais doubles as the court room for sessions of Chief Pleas. In 1987 there were thirty children at school on the island and three teachers. I visited the senior school several times, first in the winter of 1987 when the children were

making cards, covered boxes, bookmarks, etc. for the annual
Christmas fair. The school consists of one room and a store, two
pictures of Queen Elizabeth, one at her Coronation, plus a large
framed photograph of Dame Sibyl. Inside and out it looks like an
illustration for the nursery rhyme, 'Mary had a little lamb'. A
world away from the long confusing corridors where the first-year
child inevitably gets lost, numbered rooms, head master's study,
biology labs and gyms, the damp-stained walls of mobile
classrooms across wet playgrounds, of today's run-down English
comprehensives. One room, one store and fifteen children. The
teacher, like the Seigneur, sees me coming:

'We're used to being put under the microscope here. When
journalists come to see us we suggest that they come again and
talk to the children about their own jobs, it's only fair.

'We have fifteen children in this school at the moment, a
mixture of pure Sark, Sark and Channel Islands, English and
Sark and pure English. We have only one child at the moment
who is completely Sark. There are no coloured people at all, no
Asians, no minorities.

'When I first came to teach here only four of the children had
been away to England. Now it's the other way round. A confined
space means tidyness, but it's very restricting. We have no
behaviour problems here, I think the children are quieter than
English children, well mannered, but it is quite difficult to teach
all subjects because I can't be a specialist in all of them, I have to
do a lot of lesson preparation. I trained as a remedial teacher.
Alcohol is a problem and broken families. We don't have divorce
here but people split up. The worrying time for children on the
island is really between sixteen and twenty-four, there are not
many jobs. We need more money for education here but lots of
people just don't see it. All children sit the Eleven Plus, some
children pass it but they or their parents don't want to go to
Guernsey. I feel they should take the opportunity but some don't.

'My grandson was sent to Guernsey, he passed the Eleven Plus
and he was there three years and it was the most miserable years

of his life. And, Sunday mornings there was no school so he'd go down on the quay in Guernsey in the hope that some boat would be coming to Sark and, worse than that . . . he knew the Brechou boat people and if they were coming as far as Brechou he would come with them and stand on the boat and look at Sark. Stand there because he was nearer home. It was terrible, he should never have been sent but we didn't know. Education . . . they say you should make your kids go and all the rest of it. . . .

'I wouldn't want to be brought up like the Guernsey lot are. They look down on us, definitely, peasants, "You don't fight back." We say, "We're so thick? How come we won the arts and crafts for so many years?" We've won it seven, eight years now. Some people the other day they were talking about the new school curriculum and they said, "How do you do the GCSE over here?" and I said, "We don't." "Well, you're not going to be very well off for a job after, are you?" they said and I replied, "I've already got one which is more than you've got!" It does bother us sometimes but we think about it and we look at them. As a school and I think generally, Sark people of our age are much better behaved and that. We're not boasting but we're much more grown-up than them.'

'There is something about Sark schools that make them feel sort of cosy because we have got small windows, but on the mainland the schools have great panes of glass which makes the building feel bare and not as comfortable.'

'Friends that come over from England they're always saying they went and had a doss about town and you feel so, well, behind. When some other friends saw my school work . . . we're such a mixed age, we have to do a table square, it's good practice but we had to do it for the sake of the little ones. He picked this up and he saw it and he just laughed and he said, "My God! She's still doing tables." And I said, "I'm not, it's for the little ones." Don't you think that's embarrassing, when someone comes over and we're still doing that? Adjectives and pronouns and all that, I've done

121

about four or five times since I've been there, I mean we do it every term. There's always a new lot coming up so you don't get far ahead unless you're split up and we don't get split up very often. We don't work in twos, we work in thirteen upwards.'

'This photograph album, sunrise behind Cat Rock when going out fishing, I put that together when we went to London last, when we went to England on a school trip. We visited the Chelsea Pensioners and we took it so that the children could show the pensioners who hadn't been to Sark something of what Sark was like.

'What were the children like in London? Far too polite! You can never get them through doors because they stand back and let everybody else go through first. A bit dangerous on the roads, four teachers to about twelve children. It has to be that ratio because they are totally naive about London traffic and leaving belongings about. You can leave belongings where you like here and, within reason, you can pick them up later. Sark children are very much more trusting than most people, they're not street-wise at all. They're much kinder. The thing that shocked them all, dreadfully, when we first went to London was the fact that we were in a hotel in Paddington and there were gardens there and there were a couple of winos collapsed in a heap in the garden and nobody was paying any attention to them at all, which people don't in London do they? It shocked them all really badly, that's what they remembered more than anything else. It wouldn't have happened here, somebody would have taken them some-where into their home if necessary or certainly to some sort of shelter.'

'On the train going home, there were a million men and women with Marshall Field bags. There was this empty seat that people kept walking over to and not sitting down in. Next to it was a man who was dying, a bum. This guy is like starving to death. A conductor finally came to see if he was breathing. Then people just started laughing.
(STUDS TERKEL, *The Great Divide*)

'The other thing that struck them was the filthiness of London. It was just after the bin men's strike. We always take the children very carefully once into the Underground rush hour to show them how totally different life is in a crowded city. We have to carefully choose a part of the carriage where they can't be pushed out of the door. And, they are absolutely overcome by this crush of people and we make sure they experience that at least once. The other thing of course that impresses everybody is how hot everywhere is. The Planetarium, Madame Tussaud's, we take them to Selfridge's to march through it and Oxford Street and show them how big Marks and Spencer's can be as opposed to the tiny little one at Creasey's Store in Guernsey. We take them to the theatre and the children choose at least one of the things they want to see. We go to the theatre at least four times during our seven days. We go to the Zoo and to the Royal Mews, one of the carriage drivers has a friend who is the royal coachman, so we get a conducted tour round there. We see the V and A, the Natural History Museum, Westminster Abbey, the Changing of the Guard, we go to MacDonalds which they think is BLISS, walk to St Paul's, that sort of thing. You see it's interesting for them because they're not used to seeing so many people.'

'We went on a school trip to London but we didn't have any trouble from the people of London because we never met any children from London. We didn't really think about it, we were too busy wandering around. I'd like to go for a holiday again but I'd hate to live there because if I lived there I'd stay awake. Oh I know you get used to it, but you stay awake with the traffic and the lights. It's really weird, you feel like you get . . . like it was so busy and you felt squashed in and you wanted your open space and you wanted to feel free.'

'In my years there the majority of children didn't want to leave the island, their roots are there. The chidren have something we haven't got over here. I think it is a comparative smallness of numbers, that inborn background that they have, the island community are still really one big family, still very dependent on one another.'

'We all go swimming together at Petit Champs Hotel. We help the little ones. It isn't because there's a teacher there, it's just because you want to really. If there was no teacher we still would. The older ones would probably muck around more but you'd still help the younger ones.'

'I'd like to be a millionaire when I grow up, I'd drive a carriage.'

'There's been a baby boom, about nine kids at playschool and a lot more babies coming up. You feel so secure, no worries, the children know all the teachers and all the other children before they go to school. We'll still send them away if we can. Sark is a fairly unnatural environment. if they want to come back, fair enough, whether that will fit into the education system or whether we send them away later, I don't know. We were sent away lock, stock and barrel.'

# 10

# '. . . just the right size'

Mr Pye, who had for the last fifteen minutes been staring
fixedly at the approaching island, joined his hands
together beneath his chin, turned his round face to the
sky, closed his eyes, stood upon the tips of his toes, and
breathed deeply.

'It is just the right size,' he murmured. 'It will do very
nicely.'

(MERVYN PEAKE, *Mr. Pye*)

In the centre of the island, at the end of The Avenue, and
on the main road to the Church, is one of the most unique
and modern art galleries of its size, outside London. Its
exterior design is slightly reminiscent, in its atmosphere,
of XVIth century Spanish-American architecture, and is
most imposing in its simple lines, especially in the planes
of roof recession and barrel-vaulted top.

The Gallery, which it might be mentioned, was built by
island labour, was opened on August 30th by La Dame de
Serke, Mrs. R. W. Hathaway, who is keenly interested in
the venture. The opening attracted many visitors, not only
from Sark, but also from Guernsey. Sales, since the
opening, have been remarkably good.

The birth of this unique gallery, together with its
supporting art colony, should be an incentive and an
object lesson to Sark inhabitants and also to lovers of this
glorious island. Sark strives unceasingly to preserve its
natural beauties. It is hoped that the art seed, planted in
the very heart of the island, will help in its preservation,
and provide a Mecca to those whose life is spent in

translating nature, and also to those who love art and nature.

(*The Artist*, November 1933)

One of the leading St. Ives artists came to Sark to do a write-up for *The Studio*; I forget his name and the date. He was virtually speechless as I took him round the island: 'My God, the light!'

(ERIC DRAKE, letter to G. Peter Winnington, 1977)

Wednesday, a day of gold and blue and green saw the opening of the Sark Art Gallery . . . to the opening ceremony itself at three o'clock came a very mixed bevy of people. . . . La Dame looking very charming in a delightful ensemble of navy blue and white with touches of scarlet and Mrs. Drake in an elegant black crêpe de chine gown worn over a blouse of white lace with a black and white hat to match . . . Mr. Drake is to be congratulated on the materialisation of his dreams, and all real lovers of Sark will hope, with him, that that enchanting island will remain forever as unspoiled as it is today, and the Mecca of all to whom trees and flowers will ever remain more priceless possession than gold mines.

(*Guernsey Advertiser and Star*, 2 September 1933)

A number of communities of this type were being established at this time: some were as far away as the Pacific, others, such as Clough Williams-Ellis's Portmeirion experiment, as near as North Wales. The belief was that if artists could live together cheaply, free of the sordid necessity of making a living, they would produce fine work.

The Drakes settled for Sark, and in the extraordinarily short time of seven weeks a gallery was built to plans drawn up by Eric.

(JOHN WATNEY, *Mervyn Peake*)

Those [artists] like Ethel Cheesewright and William Toplis, who had made Sark their home for some time, were already well known but there were several younger artists exhibiting who had only recently arrived and [Sibyl] wished them equal success with their work. Among these was a young man of twenty-two, Mervyn Peake . . .

(BARBARA STONEY, Sybil, Dame of Sark)

'Tall, dark, good speaking voice. Attractive? Oh, God, yes, I thought so. Interesting to talk with, knew his European politics, travelled the world. Loved Sark. The point I think is that Sark people won't talk to you about Mervyn Peake because they don't remember him. In my view he did make an impact and I was not in love with him. I liked him, we were very, very great friends.'

The most outstanding picture in the exhibition, an oil painting of two Sark men playing darts in a public-house, is his [Peake's], and most of the work which attracted particular attention bore his signature. The effect of light which he brings into his pictures makes them vivid, alive and arresting, and this is particularly so in 'Darts' in which he has captured the gas-light effect in the 'pub' most impressively. The portraits of the two men make fascinating character studies.

(Guernsey Advertiser and Star, 2 September 1933)

Not all the Sarkese approved of the activities of these strange young painters, and some of the more conventional painters who had lived there for years resented the intrusion. . . . The local press was enthusiastic, for nothing so newsworthy had come to the Channel Islands since Victor Hugo had been a voluntary exile in Jersey [sic], eighty or so years earlier. Mervyn was a favourite subject of the press reports. The Guernsey Press called him an 'outstanding exhibitor' while the Star and Gazette used the words 'something approaching genius' when describing the work of this young man, 'still on the sunny side of twenty-two'. Not all the Sarkese, however, agreed with this assessment. One of them, depicted in the 'Darts' painting, threatened to sue Mervyn for making him 'look like a monkey'.

(JOHN WATNEY, Mervyn Peake)

They want, in the words of Mr. Mervyn Peake, to put 'guts' into pictures. Their pictures are powerful, grim, delineations of Sark characters. Old fishermen and farmers are portrayed just as they are, and the absence of pretence in the artists' nature and character studies is remarkable.

(*Daily Herald*, 2 May 1934)

The wild cliff scenery of the Island with its colourful caves perfectly conformed with the Romantic canons of Natural Beauty prevailing in the Victorian era, and poets of the period were inspired to extol in verse Sark's picturesque charm. . . . The fame of the Island's scenic beauty was also spread by the work of such artists as Paul Naftel, Peter Le Lievre and William Toplis; it is notable that the human inhabitants seldom figure in the paintings of these artists.

(*Fief of Sark*)

'Mervyn Peake, never knew him, had no dealings with him, he was a good artist, oh yes. Before I met Toplis I didn't know I could paint but he said, "It's in you," he said, "You can do it and it's in you and you've got it get it out." He said, "If you mix your colours don't worry about this and that, mix yellow with brown, mix your own colours, or brown and purple, whatever you want. Make the colours and look at the colours and nine out of ten times you get it exactly as you want it." I think he had private money, enough to carry on. When he died and his daughters were still living and I went to see them, one – she was getting on in her seventies – she says, "Here's my father's paint box, brushes, they're for you," and I value them, and the box has all gone rusty outside with age. "Some day you could paint with it," she said. I said, "No. If I paint with it the value's gone, that must be a hundred years old." He taught me a different world and I was taking in what he was talking about. He was a loner, some of his favourite places were the Autelets, Dixcart Bay, the natural arch and Venus Pool and Port Gorey. He said to me, "If you're painting try and get everything in your paintings." There were no figures in his paintings, landscapes.'

\*

'My father's attraction was built . . . the antithesis of Van Gogh's walk into the sunflower wilderness. He was trying to find microscopic romance in a tangible form in which there was control. Sark is a microcosm of humanity on a little granite rock, not very much more than the equivalent of a sleepy village in Sussex. My father wanted to be in charge and to make a mark, he was the shyest show-off of all. Sark gave him a sense of control, the control over the way in which he could expand an idea. A granite rock set in a greyish sea. The politics were toy-town, he had a piratical, romantic view.' (SEBASTIAN PEAKE)


'Eccentric but very nice, oh yes. I was up on Big Sark then, I used to do his [Peake's] carting. Oh God, a laugh a minute. You couldn't go round there without having a damn good laugh yourself. Very tall, and thin, dark hair.

'The Gallery was stupid, I would say. That was the time we started seeing all the weird, long-haired twits and bearded people, the one they called Jesus Christ, they were a lot of rabble really, you call them yobbos now. It was all gone in three years, I suppose. If you'd seen the pictures, oh I could paint them with a bucket of cement and throw it onto a wall, just like that, but he was good. It was splash here and splash there you know. It went in a puff of smoke like so many things that happen on Sark. Oh yes, I'm still a great believer – you go so far with Sark and Sark will turn back and say, "You go." Those who built the roof of the Gallery they've all gone by.

'Sark is an artist's paradise really, a lot of writers and artists used to come to Sark, not so much now, perhaps they can't afford it now. People lived here, it's a pity really that's gone by as well, because they were rather eccentric too.'

One does not usually associate Sark with something really modern, but anyone visiting the Sark Art Gallery at the opening of the first exhibition of the second season will find that they have stepped out from a world that is almost primitive into a realm where modernity is the very keynote.

Those who were privileged to see the first exhibition, last year, of the Sark Group's work were very impressed. Even those who did not whole-heartedly approve of the impressionistic quality of the work, were struck with the vitality, the tone and the atmosphere which this school of moderns introduced into everything they produced. And these qualities are even more apparent in this season's work, so much so that an older school of artists are beginning to realise and appreciate what they own quite frankly they do not always, in essence, understand.

(*Guernsey Gazette and Star*, 22 May 1934)

The first London Exhibition of the Sark Group, at the Cooling Galleries, New Bond Street, has attracted considerable attention – so much, in fact, that it has been found necessary to hold a fifth exhibition in Sark this summer, from September to October. . . . The portrait selected by Messrs. Cooling for display in their window, was Mervyn Peake's latest portrait, of the Prévot, Mr. Baker, looking very striking, gazing out on Bond Street!

(*Guernsey Advertiser and Star*, 19 May 1934)

November 29th, 1942. Poor dear Mr. Toplis died on Friday and is to be buried tomorrow. The old lady is bearing up wonderfully. He has had a most interesting life and his work will still live on. Unfortunately the Germans are trying to buy his paintings to take back to Germany. A German officer offered four pounds for one of his big masterpieces, they are not well off but will not part with any pictures.

(JULIA TREMAYNE, *War on Sark*)

'What saddens me more about artists is old Mr Toplis. He had two eccentric daughters and they turned those most beautiful canvasses into shelter for their hens, put them for the fowl house. They had no respect for it, for the value, no feeling. They were poor and when they wanted to keep their hens sheltered they just pierced a hole and made a roof with dozens of these old paintings of the island. There is one painting given to the island which is looked after in Guernsey, there was no place to keep it.'

The closing of the Gallery, (temporarily, as I thought at the time) due to threat of war in '38 . . . the final closing in '46 due to the after-effects of the war itself.

(ERIC DRAKE, letter to G. Peter Winnington, 1977)

'The Gallery, an absolute dead duck, it didn't last very long. I think he [Peake] was looked down on a bit by the locals, another loony artist. In art, if you want to do anything other than portraits or landscapes, the community just won't understand, you're wasting your time really.'

'My father wasn't a mixer. Charming, he couldn't help magnetising people to him, but he was distanced from both camps, indigenous and English, because he was different. The encapsulation of humanity within a tiny, confined, pliable, conquerable, finite area, that is the romantic view, like Gauguin. He went back to live on Sark with us when I was five in 1946, twelve days after the end of the Occupation. Perhaps he was waiting to come back? We left Sark in 1949, he was writing *Gormenghast*. *Mr. Pye* came out in 1953, it was remaindered. *Mr. Pye* actually wanted to control a microcosm of humanity because the scale of total humanity, the Chinese for instance, is too big.' (SEBASTIAN PEAKE)

*Mr. Pye* has languished in the shadow of the Titus trilogy, now deservedly restored in posthumous homage to the author. It is comic morality in an unflaggingly perfect mock-Edwardian style. Mr Pye stands at the head of those fictional characters, and there are many, who disrupt the status quo of a tight and smug little community.

(*Tribune* quote from Penguin edition, 1986)

'But you do not take me altogether by surprise,' he continued, 'not altogether. After all, we are not visitors. When things occur we are not the last to lay our ears to the ground – are we, dear?'

'We're not altogether backward, if that's what you mean, Arthur,' she replied.

'Not altogether,' Mr. Rice agreed. 'After all there has been very little conversation on this island for the last few months that has not been about Mr. Pye. It has been Mr. Pye this, and Mr. Pye that, morning, noon and night – . . . .'
(MERVYN PEAKE, *Mr. Pye*)

'Two things have happened I suppose in this century on Sark. The Occupation and the filming of the Peake book, *Mr Pye*.'
(RICHARD PELERINE, anthropologist)

'You imagine the effect on Sark of sixty new people, all self-assured and good in their field, all new people to come to Sark! It was so exciting, suddenly there were all these people here and they were all normal people.'

'I read the book while I as working on a film in India, a rather odd book to read in India. I went on a recce, traipsed round the island on bicycles, I was thinking it looked like jolly hard work because there were so little facilities and you had to do everything on bicycles so, for my department [art director/props], it looked like a nightmare. It was filmed in La Jaspellerie and there's no road to it, well there is a track but it's tractors or nothing.
  'Their attitude was, you film people you can come in here and shout around, throw your money around and tell us what to do and we'll do it but we'll do it in our way and in our own time. You know what it's like, "For God's Sake! we need some of that," you must run and get them but they ambled off, had a beer. . . .'

'The film crew weren't exactly wonderful, they didn't treat the islanders like islanders, they wanted to own the island for their film and that was it and leave it. They expected you to do something exactly when they asked for it. They came in March and talked to some of the islanders and then they started filming in June. To get a job you just turned up, they said, "Do you fancy coming to do this and this and this?" We got a morning off school, others got off more because they had a part. If you play the film now I can point myself out, I'm not just a dot in the crowd, I'm in various bits, I went down to Port du Moulin for the beach party. You had to get your parents' permission, I didn't know about it, they had to 'phone to say you were allowed in case something happened. The beach party scene was over three nights, we got paid, it was pouring down with rain. We just sat in the tent singing because it was raining and filmed on the other nights. There was a lot of waiting. We were dressed up, bowl hair cut, took weeks to grow out, shorts, pair of yachting shoes, a guernsey and a little blue cap. Some of us had absolutely shaven hair and half of us looked like gangsters.'

'Extras? I remember some boys on bicycles which was a nightmare for me, I had to give them out bicycles which were always falling to pieces, roaring through and crashing into things, then we had to buy more bicycles. We wrote-off more bicycles. . . . I can't tell you. The crew all had bicycles and I think out of twenty-five bikes there were fifteen write-offs, quite an achievement. All the crew got terribly boyish and we used to take the mudguards off and go faster and faster and tighten the back brake, skids and everything, of course we were always crashing.'

'I'm glad I was in it now but I'd never get involved in that line again. You think Sark is insane but the film industry is insanity taken to extremes. So manic, so hysterical – the production assistant was bonkers – they weren't happy unless there was a crisis. One phoned up here at four in the morning about something that was happening that afternoon! We did have some fun, though, because in the end we learned how to screw the system, which was not to get involved . . . you basically disappeared off with somebody and went off and had fun with them, usually it involved some drinking or boat trips.'

'Sixty people coming over to this rock with torches and bicycles and finding they could only have baths on Tuesdays and Wednesdays. I think there was a lot of, "What is this place?" when they first got here. It's hard work on any film set and in Sark everything is virtually impossible.'

'We couldn't film on Sunday, you couldn't ride on the tractors, none of us were allowed to drive a tractor and there were never enough tractors to go round, other things had priority. We were kept in our place, they wouldn't run for us, I rather respected them, it was rather nice. The weather was pretty bad, we got soaked. If you forgot a prop – in films they always forget things – it was two miles on a bicycle in the wind and the rain to get it if you could carry it. . . . Haversacks, I remember. It was very hard work. They'd ask for a picture and all the things were on the trailer and the trailer was the other side of the island and it was seven at night and he'd gone to the pub or somewhere else . . . it would take me three hours to get the paints out of the trailer then get home to paint the picture that was being filmed next morning. . . . My camera fell out of my bicycle basket, it was loaded to the gunnels with props and things I needed. We used to go down to the Dixcart flat out on those ruts and it jumped out and fell into the wheel. I was cut all over and battered to pieces, I could hardly move, the doctor couldn't believe the accident rate among the film crew.

'We were allowed to take a Citroen 2CV and film from the back of it because it had a very good suspension, very smooth, but we weren't allowed to drive the car, the distributor had to go. It was pulled by a tractor, so . . . you had a tractor towing a car, towing a cart. This bizarre convoy would streak around Sark, people running after it for the chase scenes.

'The logistics of the beach party scenes were unbelievable. The beach was only accessible by a mile and a half of cliff path, really steep, through a jungle, and we had to take down there enough food and booze for three days and the harmonium. Everybody carried things down and we had a boat delivering the heavy stuff. They were very nice, they put up with everything very well. When it rained we hid in the caves and they couldn't have suffered more or been nicer about it really. If I ever wanted to do a film about rural England in the fifties, or the war, I think I'd go to Sark to do it.'

*

'My son went to help with *Mr. Pye* and he said he's never roared so much in all of his life. He really, really enjoyed it, they had the time of their lives and acting sometimes. Definitely did the world of good to Sark, money-wise. They came at a time when there weren't all that amount of visitors, they came at the end of the winter, just at the right time and of course they paid so well. They commandeered the Dixcart Hotel and La Jaspellerie. We thoroughly enjoyed the film as far as the crowds were concerned, picking out people we knew. I don't think anybody was really impressed with much else but the film has done a world of good, more visitors.'

It seemed impossible that the island could be turned upside down in so short a time. Age-old enmities, age-old feuds, were melting away in the warmth of his sunbeams. A new spirit was abroad in Sark – so much so that old friends of the island who were returning for Easter were amazed to receive as they disembarked at the stone jetty, so effusive a welcome. 'There's something different about Sark,' they would say, 'it's almost as though they like us.'
(MERVYN PEAKE, *Mr. Pye*)

'My job was holding the horses out of scene, driving, catching horses. It was a lot of fun and it had a lot of consequences, girls going off with the sound technicians . . . a lot of people obviously interacted with the film crew and a lot of the crew started to go out with people over here. I was sitting out on these rocks with a girl who was flirting like mad with the director and we were sitting out on these rocks and the tide was coming in. . . .'

*Mr. Pye* was filmed in and around the tenement house, Jaspellerie. It stands on its own up a cart track from the Dixcart Hotel and looks down to Dixcart Bay. It is not a sensational house, there are houses on Sark more beautiful, and its closeness to the easiest bay means it is, in Sark terms, busy, but there is an atmosphere around Jaspellerie that pulls you.

Things happen in this house; empty now, one feels it's waiting.

135

The famous privateering Slowleys lived here in the seventeenth century, and it was here in October 1942 that the Commandos came knocking at the door:

> They went across the Dixcart Valley, through thick gorse and bracken, and came on a little house, known as La Jaspellerie, standing by itself in the middle of a lawn. They broke a pane in a French window on the ground floor, under the catch, and rushed inside with their guns at the ready. . . . A woman came out in her dressing gown. She asked, 'Is the house on fire?' It turned out that her name was Mrs Pittard, and that she was now living alone, her husband having died a few months earlier.

*Islands in Danger* tells the rest of the story. Julia Tremayne's *War on Sark* gives us the detail that makes it live:

> October 31st, 1942. Frances [Mrs Pittard] made me a little ginger cake, she came and had a cup of tea and was quite perky and bright but at 10.30 that night the Gestapo, or Military Police, stormed the Jaspellerie and took her off somewhere, no one knows where or why.
> November 13th, 1942. There is still no news about Mrs. Pittard, no one knows if she is in Guernsey, France or Germany and worse still no one knows what she has been taken away for.

After an impromptu drinking session with the much-loved English woman who ran the Dixcart Hotel until 1988, I borrowed the key to the house and I went up there alone that winter morning and let myself in.

Discarded film cans, damp double mattresses leaned against the walls, the discoloured cream wooden doors of cupboards in the wall left hanging open, broken bannisters, bare littered boards, dirty, curtainless windows . . . all of it, drunk or sober, somehow absolutely wonderful. Jaspellerie is the sort of house that one imagines oneself living in: standing at the sink, how the feet fit into the identations on the lino; looking into the courtyard, washing on the line; opening the tall French windows onto the planked colonnaded verandah in the summer, stuffing the same verandah doors with newspapers in the autumn and winter to keep out the wind.

One would of course be an entirely different person, serene and quietly organised, the sort of writer who works in the morning then goes for a walk in the afternoon rather than creeping back into bed. The beauty and peace of Sark, that sense of being out of call or cry, so quickly eclipsed by a working knowledge of life on the island in this decade, is distilled in Jaspellerie's empty rooms and overgrown garden. Jaspellerie is Little Gidding out of Howards's End. Thank God Swinburne missed it.

'When we took the wallpaper off one of the rooms in that house there was a mural of a palm tree obviously painted by Peake. They don't really like Mervyn Peake, he was rather eccentric I believe, an odd ball, a loner.'

'The stuntman trained the horse that was meant to have bolted. It's all right, I seen it in the carriage after. Half the old people they didn't want to be bothered with the film, taking up all their time. Everybody said it was a load of rubbish, the signature tune and the shot of Sark when it opened, that was the best bit. Mervyn Peake, I knew he built the gallery, I knew he was a bit of a whacko as well. He sort of ran round the place with horns sticking out of his head. I know someone who has a painting he did of her when she was younger, her daughter looks exactly the same now, sentimental value. I think if they'd made a documentary with all the money they spent on the film it would have done a lot better.'

> Mervyn was on target in *Mr. Pye*. While Sark is seraphic to visitors it can become daemonic for some people who choose to live there. (ERIC DRAKE, *Peake Studies*)

'We're now all experts on film so it wouldn't be the same again. I would have loved to have been a publican, it seemed to me I would earn my £20 for the day then I would go and spend £22 in the pub. Everybody was doing the same thing, transferring money from the film crew to the pub. There wasn't really a special place we all met, the only time everyone was together was for the party at the end.'

'We had a party at the end in a big marquee on the lawn of the Jaspellerie. The director made a speech, everybody got very drunk and it went on all night, people still around at dawn.'

'I remember the party, some people had to be helped to it as well as from.'

'No one read it, I only sat through the first episode. Maybe because we'd all seen it being made that was enough? I've heard a few nice things about it. I've never heard anyone talk about Mervyn Peake, the only people I've ever heard were some people talking at La Moinerie who used to live next to Mervyn Peake and said they used to go round to his house and have painting parties in his house, painting the walls.'

'As you'd expect they are terribly insular, they value their quality of life, they haven't got a lot of respect for those who go off all the time. There's a lot of secret life goes on. You'd think in a tiny place, in three months, one would have got to know it all but in fact I didn't. There were whole pockets that I didn't really know anything about. There's no crime on Sark, I'll say that for it, everyone knows everyone else too well. If you did live on Sark you would write something like *Gormenghast*, it's sort of Gothic and mysterious too, isn't it? I never felt I got anywhere near the real power pulse of the island, I mean it certainly wasn't the Seigneur but the Dame ran the whole place, she was really in command from what one hears.

'It's very secretive, whole pockets I didn't have anything to do with. All the hotel owners are outsiders, and the people who work in them are outsiders, we didn't really get to grips with the Chief Pleas or anything like that. The Seigneur, he has a lot of power, you can't even settle on Sark without his say. He and his wife were terribly helpful, they couldn't have done more for the film, tremendous energy. You know what films are like, you're the biggest act in town.

'*Mr. Pye* is all about community and getting together and outsiders. *Mr. Pye* is quite a condemnation of Sark in itself, isn't it? I mean, he's hounded to death because he's different.'

# 11

# *Dancing with Juliet*

In summer 1988 I take the two children and the baby out to Sark. Once more we are the only guests, we cook our meals in the old man's kitchen and eat, surrounded by the empty tables, in the dining room, watched over by Dame Sibyl on the sideboard.

On our first morning we are given two mackerel for breakfast, caught by a relation so extended that I cannot gather who it is. The old man collects the water, watches wrestling, feeds the birds, chatters on: other summers – 'The Germans peeled beetroot and ate them like apples, we used to trade spuds for whisky' – better weather, midnight swimming, women in long dresses. . . .

On that first day it is the smell of Sark – dust and horse dung – that strikes one, the sense, quite suddenly, of being very far away; the quiet, sun setting through the stunted pine trees; the clear night sky full of brilliant stars. The children and I stand outside our bedrooms looking for a long time. I sleep with the baby in the familiar little wooden room, the children talk into the night – 'I'm going to wear my bathing suit underneath my clothes'. I go to sleep to the sound of their voices coming through the tongue-and-grooved boards behind my head.

The evening primroses have been rooted out, leaving an expanse of blank earth edged by small myrtle and veronica bushes surrounded by the Germans' roll of wire. Shamrock and violets planted by the old man's wife have long since gone. A solitary campion blooms on the bare earth and he waters it. Nothing else has changed apart from a new notice typed on a piece of card in the outside bathroom: 'Please do not wash clothes in the bath due to damage caused by zips.'

We have been here a week and are on nodding, smiling and assorted platitude terms with other holidaymakers around Beauregard. A rather nervous man, here to win a bet, works as a cartographer in the Arctic, explains to us what happens when an iceberg turns right upside down. A lyrical single lady who used to pretend she was a mermaid wanders in and joins us for an hour or so in the empty dining room and talks about the poetry she wrote yesterday whilst sitting on a rock. A forlorn-looking woman with a toothbrush and a shower cap tells us that she came to Sark seven or nine years ago and that 'It doesn't seem the same, does it? Isn't what it was.'

Living on my own here with the children has its moments, many of which are grim. It's complicated fixing a lolling baby to a bicycle, passers-by point out his list, going downhill he is sometimes sick over the side. Sark with small children is very much like life in the Hindu Kush. A carrycot strapped to the back of a bicycle with monkey clips is easily caught in brambles and sends the unwilling cyclist – it wasn't his turn – upside down into a bush. When I cycle over something soft it is frequently my handbag, and getting back from beaches is often worse than getting to them. Things that fitted together reasonably in the morning have all gone haywire by the afternoon; a black monkey clip discarded carelessly in the heat of the moment is very much like a piece of wet seaweed; the carrycot comes off the back of the bike again when it slips through a useless piece of string.

We have no money and no news but empty days begin to lull us. We establish, as one day falls into another, a system of treats that passes as routine. In the evenings we push the baby in his pyjamas across the lane to the Le Grand Beauregard. Outside this once great house we sit on wobbling benches and eat chips. Completely fed up with asking leading questions about Sark, I drink with the iceberg man and anyone else not put off by ashtrays filled with Coca Cola or a baby who takes aim and fires with small bits of half-digested bread.

Our most intimate and interesting friend is already widely celebrated on the island, though he has only just arrived. He has a tin leg with gears and, in the spirit of the La Trobes, gets up and down the exhausting descent to Grand Grève at La Coupée without fuss. We walk with him across fields, down the track that leads to the tenement, Le Vieux Port. Past the stone pig sty; past the ducks some of whom were poisoned when the farmer sold a piece of his land for building – the new owners sprayed weed killer which washed down the hill into their water; past the dark byre where I first met the farmer, a tall stooped man standing in the darkness there. Other meetings, other conversations, wandering down the track to find him, waiting whilst he beds a calf.

Dung heaps, pitch forks, old machinery rusting in the hedge. Through the yard, past the dairy, a hedgehog snuffles about beneath the washing line. It was just about here that, one November, I came cheek to cheek with a slaughtered pig swinging in the darkness above a zinc bucket of blood.

Up through the valley past Port à la Jument, gleaming windows, herbaceous borders, a tenement that's been done up. . . . Tin-leg talks of what it was like up at Oxford, older than the other students, at university after the war. Much to the fascination of all children in the vicinity he takes his leg off to swim, and has already achieved the highest tourist honour – 'Oh dear. Here we are disturbing your peace again' – of being mistaken for a Sarkee.

Summertime Sark, the village swarms. The day jars, as you queue in a non-biodegradable Crimplene swamp for a pack of Ultra Pampers that cost a third as much again. Money is the only currency now and even the money – the mill on the coins, the cow – seems a fiction, a travesty, a lie:

After the war all that remained was jet tourism among the ruins, resulting in phenomena like the appalling pollution of the Mediterranean and the Aegean. Claude Lévi-Strauss observes in 1974 that so full is the world now of its own garbage that 'journeys, those magic caskets full of dreamlike promises, will never again yield up their treasures untarnished. . . . The first thing we see as we travel round the world is our own filth, thrown into the face of mankind.' Thus 'the mad passion for travel books,

they create the illusion of something which no longer exists
but still should exist.'

(PAUL FUSSELL, Abroad)

Today's children hack away at their parents' morale in the
galleon-gloom of the Mermaid Tavern. We cycle at speed
through puddles, dodge around walkers who, with Pakamaks
over rucksacks, look like hunchbacks in the rain. The shops are
crammed, everyone is busy, a breakdown at the bakery, jokes in
the newly enlarged supermarket about auctioning one of
yesterday's brown loaves.

'If it carries on another twenty years with the change there has
been this last twenty it will be completely different. When I see
... what I can remember ... you take from going down to the
Manoir, the amount of houses built there ... at one time there
was just the doctor's house, the next one to it and then there was
La Chalet, two cottages, Rose Bud and Rose Cottage, on the
other side there was nothing at all. In the Avenue there was only
one shop, where the supermarket is now, there was none of the
others, it was completely empty. I mean when you see the shops
and houses ... and yet they still say there are no more
inhabitants than there were before. There's a long time we
haven't had a census but I think the Seigneur knows everybody
living on the island, I don't. Years ago people didn't want as
many rooms as they do now. I mean you get a couple just getting
married and they want two or three bedrooms.'

'Just little glimpses of that peasant survival economy in terms of
architecture, talking to the old people. The indigenous vernacu-
lar architecture, the way it was built and how the buildings were
sited. How can you expect a Sarkee, with hundreds of years
involved in farming – basically a peasant and I don't mean that in
a derogatory sense at all, in the highest sense – how can you
expect him to take the aesthetic standpoint that you or I might
take because they now happen to be the temporary guardians of
what is potentially a very beautiful building? Why should they

see things in that way? Therefore those parts of the island will just inevitably disappear. It's the natural inclination of the whole of our culture to become a sort of suburban landscape, and suburbia, in the case of Sark, that's death.

'We were in Majorca twice in the last five years and you go into little villages there, superb. Kept the character, none of this ghastly twentieth-century suburbanist ... you look into little courtyards, their plants and those china ceramic tiles as a contrast to those sort of matt pinky colour, and that's just ordinary people. That's not trendy designer people from the big city, that's ordinary people and yet the British seem incapable of that. We have in history done all sorts of wonderful things and shown all sorts of wonderful characteristics but one that we don't have is any sort of natural ability to design and to value our environment and so Sark's up the creek. It's gone, the whole top of the island doesn't interest me at all, actually it upsets me, it just has nothing!

'As I started to value these things and pay attention to them so they were already being eroded. You take what used to be the baker's shop, the green wooden shed which was I suppose, extremely ill-designed, unsuitable for the job and so on and so on but look what's gone up in its place, the next sort of epoch and now it looks like a small supermarket, unbelievable! I don't doubt that it's more convenient and you can go in there and get food cheaper and faster but. . . .'

The Avenue is changing again, with the removal of the old cottage where Philip le Feuvre used to live. It was not exactly the prettiest structure on the road, and I have spent many years trying to make sure it was not in photographs I took of the Avenue for one reason or another!

The house did not take long to bring down, as it was one of the old wooden-framed houses with a corrugated iron cladding, but it did contain a cheerful message from the past, from one Jean Millet in 1896 – his name, the date, and 'ta-ra-ra boom de-hay' written in broad pencil on one of the planks!

The JCB was used to level the site and remove the last of
the garden though the sycamore tree is being retained.
(*Guernsey Evening Press*, 'News From Sark', December 1988)

Tourists in Pakamaks snap the Sark ambulance, an old white
caravan with a red cross pulled by a tractor. One autumn when I
arrived on Sark on the late boat the ambulance was at the
harbour. A foreign journalist – who thought he was in a folk
museum? Who was just doing his job? – took pictures as a
stretcher case was lowered gently onto the boat, and more
pictures of a middle-aged woman who had accompanied the
ambulance and was standing wiping her eyes.

'I do minor surgery here, fish hooks and cycling accidents. I was
once cycling down the hill by the school when a cyclist in front of
me came off. "I'm the doctor," I told him, "I came as soon as I
could." Everything happens at night. I get called out for all sorts
of things. I deliver calves. Just after I arrived I was called to the
Coupée, a girl had jumped or fallen. I was taken round by boat, I
took my bag, I had no idea what to expect. She had fallen half-
way, shingle had broken the fall, no broken bones but a mass of
internal injuries. The Flying Christine took her to hospital in
Guernsey.

'No one here likes going away to hospital, particularly the old
people. Fear, they don't like the sea and you have to learn to
overrule them. The older people feel if they go to hospital they
won't come back, they forget about the ones that do come back.'

'I last went to Guernsey in January and I don't intend to go
again. I'm too old and not terribly fit and I go down too quick. I
like being at home, I'm happy here.

'I have cereal for breakfast and two pieces of toast, tea time I
might have a couple of bread and butters, I might have a little tin
of fish, sardines. I've got apples, put them in the oven, what I like
best with potatoes is washed then boiled in their jackets. There's
little toasties, poached eggs, sometimes lunch time I say, "Oh I

can't be bothered", then I like to sit down and have a rest. I watch the one o'clock news then as soon as the *Neighbours* come on it shuts off bang. I play the radio in the morning then I've got a cassette you know, I listen to all sorts. I've got a lovely one that's "Scottish Airs", seventy minutes to play both sides.

'After my wife died I thought I was going, I couldn't walk to the village. I went to Guernsey to stay with relations, the fuss. "You're not to go down there, too many cars about. We're going out in the car this afternoon. . . ." I could scream because I have never liked going out and going round and round sitting down all the time. They helped me in and out and I used to think, "Wait till I get back to Sark!" When I got back I used to go a little way up the road and back again and I used to think, "I'm getting better," and then I walked up to the village. I'm going without a stick now, it was pure determination.

'In midsummer we have an outing for the old and not so old, they take all the old people out. We used to go in the evenings and finish up at the island hall but this last two years we go on a Sunday afternoon. Last year we went to Petit Champs Hotel for a cream tea, we called in at the Seigneurie and had some drinks, lemonade, and this year we had a walk over the Coupée and went out to Little Sark.

'It's better going on living in the same place, you think she's still here and sometimes you don't realise she's dead. It's worse in the winter, long evenings. I read travel books, I get them from jumble sales, I wish we had a better library. Dick Francis, Kingsley Amis, lots of books here I've read twice. Still learning from gardening books, you have to fathom out who's right. The doctor, if he come up this way, might call in but if I see him in the village, "How are you? All right?"'

'I have many difficult decisions because this is an island. Whether to charter the St John's ambulance boat, Flying Christine or wait until the morning. The Sarkese are so courteous and don't want to bother the doctor, they have home medicines, and knowing people I am able to prescribe less. They rarely call the doctor out at all but the visitors are terrible. I was once summoned down to La Sablonnerie on Little Sark, called to a hotel guest who had a sore throat. I was having lunch and by the time I got down there she had finished hers and was sitting up drinking coffee. I get called out to yachts too. It can be quite frightening. I was once taken out to a boat where a man had a ruptured appendix, there was nothing I could do but drink brandy, waiting in the harbour at Havre Gosselin until help came.'

'There was no nurse on the island in those early days. I'd done midwifery during the war but I didn't want to take full responsibility and I went to help the doctor. Some children on Sark now, I hear they're married and have children of their own while I helped to bring their parents into the world. I also helped when people were dying.

'Someone asked for me. I sat up nights with the old woman. I remember the first night the little house was spotless and the son, he had done it all. She was spotless on a feather bed and she was incontinent yet her bedding was white as snow, absolutely wonderful. A big woman, her nighties and bedjackets, he did it all, perfect. She had her bedroom in a little sitting room and we laid a lovely fire when I got there. I sat there with just the firelight and the door wide open, most enormous spiders in the firelight, I was frightened but I contained myself. I sat up with her for about three weeks before she passed away. As an English person, I felt it was a privilege to be asked to help, it wasn't a chore. It was almost a sin to put that dear soul into the ground with what her son had brought to put on her, so beautiful the clothes and she without a sign of a bed sore.'

'Everyone knows each other here so intimately that it's difficult to keep necessary secrets and confidences. In a strange way I have found being a doctor on Sark easier philosophically. People die, then one is losing a friend as much as a patient, but knowing people well is such a bonus.

'There are strains and stresses living in a small community. Sleeping problems, anxiety and depression. Widows. And I worry about the eccentrics living here alone, it's only feasible when they are well and a double blow, if they get too ill to stay, to send someone to Guernsey. Guernsey seems like Siberia. Babies are born on Guernsey these days, there have been one or two narrow scrapes, they should go to Guernsey a month before they're due but it isn't always as neat as that.

'I have a sliding scale for prescription charges. I know what people can afford and if prices have to go up then patients inevitably go down. Requests for repeat prescriptions are left for me in the outer surgery, sometimes it's difficult to interpret what people want, a note on a bottle, "Thank you". I leave the prescriptions down at La Rendezvous on the Avenue for them to collect.

'There are problems here, loneliness. One partner likes living on the island and the other doesn't, sometimes one member of a couple is presenting symptoms but that may not be the person you treat. It's hard to be off-duty, of course, and knowing people well does increase the heartache. What I've had to do is to make do and mend, learn to make decisions without any colleagues to discuss with or support me, and learn to accept some things as they are. It is a privilege to work here. I retire at the end of the year but have decided to stay on. It is a privilege, it's their island and one must adapt as much as possible.'

Outside the Seigneurie, waiting carriage drivers swop news of the coming weather, shirt sleeves now but trouble later. Talk of gale-force winds, of fishermen moving their boats to the safety of Grève de la Ville. By afternoon, 'One big eye, one big ear', the island hums with talk of hurricane.

Above the beach at Grand Grève, which blisters in the heat, a crying child says she is frightened of being stuck on the island and wants her parents to take her home. The uninitiated who have left their bikes by the litter bins where flying ants crawl and swarm collect them now and cycle swiftly home. Tents are struck at Beauregard, the woman in the shower cap and the iceberg man have fled.

Rain and tearing wind in the night and in the morning mist so thick that we can't see the field in front of the house, nor the Pilcher Monument nor Brechou. The island is quiet, no one ventures out unless they have to, a pig of a day.

'How many people trying to do the same thing as you,' says a farmer, comforting a young girl who's trying to make a cake. The Produce Show is a big event on the calendar. No boats in this weather, more talk and speculation, what will happen if the judges can't get across. . . . We drink sloe gin in the kitchen, our taped interview interspersed with, 'Don't open the oven door', 'Put it on the rack this way', 'Get it out with the spatula not the knife'. The entry form on the table between us is checked and checked again.

The farmer usually makes a killing with his mangels – 'Couldn't fault them, gave them full marks' – but the sponge is a more volatile beast than the mangel. 'Just like me picking my roots up today,' he continues, but it isn't: 'One year my wife made a dozen before she could get the one she wanted.'

'We can't judge our own flowers here, favouritism, a small place. People used to say to me, "Look, it's no use to put it in if he wins everything," but I wonder. You see you're allowed one entry per person and we had lots and lots of dahlias and I tried to go out to win every first prize. We have our entries in sealed envelopes like a pack of cards. We had every first prize in the arrangement of dahlias for effect. We had first, second and third for five different classes, they didn't study it right you see. Sometimes I've been up at the hall and I've looked at the entries and somebody's said, "Well, I thought that one would have won," and I'd said, "Yes. If they'd done it properly, they would have won, the blooms are better than mine but the presentation's wrong."'

'The Produce Show was wonderful, everyone praying for fine weather the days before because if we had a gale it damaged the things to come.

'We had a very old, neglected fig tree – every year La Dame always had first prize for her plate of figs. I nursed my few figs, I wrapped them up in ladies' tights or stockings because the birds would eat them before they were ripe, you see. We had to have, I think it was, eight identical figs on a plate and I won first prize and La Dame presented me with the prize and she was lovely about it. The Produce Show was very exciting, I have my last programme and I show it to the people in England and try to inspire them. It's so beautifully done on Sark, so beautifully laid out.'

Today is the second day of Sark's annual agricultural show, the grand autumn show. Despite the wind and rain and the cancelling of the boats bringing judges from Guernsey, the show opened in time. Thanks to early gale warnings a large part of the entries arrived safely in the island hall on Wednesday night ahead of the tempest. Even those who had to battle their way through the driving rain on Thursday morning succeeded in getting their exhibits to the table more or less intact and produced an extremely colourful show. For the first time since 1969 the boats were cancelled and the Guernsey judges couldn't get to Sark but both residents and visitors rose to the occasion and there were two judges for each of the seven sections before 9.30 a.m. The committee are extremely grateful to them all for their help. The president and the secretary assured everyone that this was not the reason for their resignations at the presentations, that they had warned everyone that this would happen on previous occasions.

(GUERNSEY RADIO NEWS)

Safe inside the island hall the exhibits are inspected and discussed. A cucumber cut into an alligator, a Roman cameo brooch done in icing sugar, a cake like a map of Australia which includes a kangaroo with something in its pouch. I look and feel that people watch me looking, daren't make any notes. More than any other island event the Produce Show is sacrosanct, the island establishment asserting itself, not the Brigadier and the Seigneur who both did well, but the strength of the women, perhaps unconsciously, closing ranks, discussing the consistency of jam.

'A treat not to hear the wind.' A day that dawns in sea mist and storm, calms, as the old man said it would, by the afternoon. The sea is still. The old man talks of nights when it was too hot to have a shirt on your back, let alone a jacket. . . .

Late in the afternoon sit in weak sunshine to watch the dismantling of the Produce Show. Guernsey sweaters much in evidence as men and women who belong work together in the island hall. Carriages and bicycles cautiously pass the tractor and trailer where a man and a boy are stacking up the trestles. This has all been done before and is done carefully by size and takes a long time. As the tables are stacked the produce is carried a hundred yards or so up to the church. Off go the marrows and mangels. A very frail, grey-haired woman carries eggs to the church on a sagging paper plate.

The church is full for Harvest Festival, the congregation well turned out, rows of bicycles leant against the graveyard wall, squeeze in at the back, Hermès scarves, Viyella shirting, a sea of navy blue.

'Notices first of all. The most important notice is to you for your gifts which are all around us and some which you are hugging but not for much longer, and all those who worked so hard yesterday to decorate the church, flowers. . . We are all enjoying it, thank you very much indeed and thank you all for coming today. We will auction the produce outside after the service if it's not raining, it won't be raining, so do stay behind after the service and bid generously.'

September 2nd, 1944. Our Harvest Festival was on Sunday and the church was packed with all sorts of sundries and vegetables galore. A padre came over from Guernsey for three days. The veg and oddments were sold by auction the next day. Mr. H. sent a whole packet of

151

candles and several dozen matches. I went to the sale hoping
to buy a candle but they were sold in twos and threes and
each candle worked out about three or four shillings each
and matches (one box), about the same. A small tablet of
Lux soap brought 52 marks (£5.2s.6d.) think of it, ordinary
prices in peace-time about 3d. or 4d. a tablet. The vegetables
brought unheard-of prices.

(JULIA TREMAYNE, *War on Sark*)

'We still manage to do it in the old way, like when I was a child.
Most festivals these days are all tins and packets, we send our
stooks of wheat to Jersey for their festivals. I remember the days
when there were sacks of potatoes.'

'During the singing of the next hymn, "We plough the Fields and
Scatter", I'm going to ask those children who are still nursing
their gifts of produce to bring them up.'

The organ plays the familiar chords. I remember unexpectedly
Heaney's 'Scattered flesh of labourers', reminded as I stand here
of how we all take ourselves with us wherever we go. Confident
singing. Babies who've chewed through the order of service
squeak between the verses. Bunches of maize decorate the lights
at the end of each pew. Dahlias, first, second and consolation,
trimmed carrots and polished tomatoes, grapes, bracken and
kindling. The red, white and blue irises and carnations of the
wreath laid for the French commandos; graves gone to grass,
graves with empty jam jars. Someone reads a poem by John
Betjeman about harvest mice, the atmosphere of the church
suddenly not much different from the atmosphere at the island
dog show.

'The dog with the waggiest tale, the dog most like its owner, best
pedigree, best mongrel dog, obedience, agility, obstacles. There
was a little sausage dog called Chipper, he couldn't get over
anything so the lady had to lift him over everything. There was a
bath of water to put them through but half the dogs wouldn't go
in so a girl jumped in the bath. The ladder was rocky, not really

meant for big excited dogs, they had to run up and go down the other side. Fancy dress, one as a beach dog with string Y-fronts and a sun visor carrying a bucket with a Bonio in it. The sausage dog was a waiter with a waistcoat and the owner was dressed the same carrying a tray with a glass on it. The prize was a dog dressed up as Pedigree Chum. There was a hot dog with ketchup and baps on each side and a postal strike dog with parcels and postcards. There was a really menacing dog called Hugo and suddenly over the loud speaker, "Can someone catch Hugo please and put him on a piece of string," Hugo was a Bassett Hound. There was another Bassett, every time he barked his bottom shot up, very noisy, and a dog about 10cm called Nugget. There were ladies in track suit bottoms and red wellingtons, grannies who couldn't run very fast, everybody was there, it was a big occasion.'

The vicar corrects the balance: 'God and Jesus expect us to say "thank you" . . . I wonder if we're honest, let's try being honest today . . . most of us are guilty of not giving thanks. . . .'

> September 20th, 1942. Our little church looks beautiful and another harvest festival has come round. The Thanksgiving service was very saddened by a prayer being offered by the vicar for the evacuees leaving for Germany and all the new-laid eggs sent to the Festival are to be hard-boiled and given to the people as they leave the island.
>
> (JULIA TREMAYNE, *War on Sark*)

'When you came in that door this morning I wonder if you really said, "thank you God" for your gifts? Those simple words, "Thank you very much". . . . There are some who say as long as you feel thankful it doesn't matter whether you say it or not, while I think the opposite this morning, we ought to thank God and we ought to be more thankful . . . there are a lot of people who haven't got enough, four out of five children don't have enough food. Somebody mentioned it this morning, the tragedies of Bangladesh, Eritrea in Sudan, Mozambique . . . the list is almost never-ending of people who haven't got enough and it's our responsibility. I feel it would be marvellous if each one of us today could give something to societies who are sending food to these people. The hundred and fifty people here could save one hundred and fifty children's lives.'

On Bank Holiday Monday the keen assemble outside the Rendezvous for the 'Discover the Real Sark Walk'.

'I'd put your bike over there if I were you. Now, does anyone want to leave anything at the shop?'

'My husband.'

'That wasn't very nice, was it? But you're going to be outnumbered by the look of it, nearly all women this morning.'

Despite or because of the vile weather, our entirely English group introduce each other, talk and laugh in a most unEnglish way. As we wait for late arrivals our positions in the hierarchy of visitors to Sark are, however, unequivocably established. How many holidays each has had on Sark, self-catering, hotel, tent? Staying with relations is two-star, staying with friends just one. Who knows who and how well they know them – 'I went there for a drink with Derek Jacobi' – first names flourished, planted like flags.

'You may have to carry the buggy occasionally, a bit rocky on the road. This walk is for charity, for the medical equipment fund, once we get our new medical centre there'll be all sorts of things wanted.'

Oblivious of Siberian cross-winds a couple arrive on a tandem, seriously long Pakamaks and shorts. They are obviously going for the La Trobe Scrambling Mantle. Yes, they went to the lecture on sea anemones yesterday, and yes, they already knew about the anemones. They're off to the Gouliot Caves this afternoon to study the lichens, they need a low tide for this, yes, they've checked.

'Everybody been to the toilet? This is Bank Holiday so watch out, bikes, tractors, people in the middle of the road . . .'

'Do we pass a toilet?'

'It's over the hedge I'm afraid. . . . Now you all know you're in Sark, of course. We're a little feudal island about 1 by 3, quite high-sided, three or four hundred feet and forty miles of coastline round the bottom, indented with valleys. We have a Seigneur who's our lord and master, have our own court, parliament called Chief Pleas, we have two constables. Any man on the island can be a constable, no training whatsoever, he goes from assistant to full constable then retires. He's a working man of the island but he seems to manage very well. They don't have a uniform, we don't get a lot of crime, only a bit of drunkenness. We had rather nasty Saturdays so we decided to close the pubs, open just lunch time and evening, and we seem to have got over that little problem. All the drunks go to Herm now, sorry Herm. Now you're standing in what's known as the Avenue. . . .

'This is quite a historical area. This was called the Arsenal and that was where they kept the small arms and ammunition when they were fighting the French. Continually the island were fighting the French, that's why it was colonised because Guernsey and Jersey were always being attacked by the French boats coming out of France. . . . Now we've got our little prison, they say, "You don't keep people in there, do you?" Yes we do! No windows, not that comfortable but you can be in there for three days, then you come up before our Seneschal which is the magistrate and then you're fined. We've just put the fines up but if it was anything serious you'd be sent to Guernsey. People in Victorian days, they came over to see the Silver Mines, a little day out for Victorian ladies. Can you look at the prison and see what they would have nicknamed it . . . look at the shape of it . . . ?'

Even the tandem riders are nonplussed. Some of us pretend we didn't catch the question, others stare hard at the shape of the prison, rain dribbles down our necks.

'No? No takers? The Tea Caddy.'

The prison, lynch-pin of many a documentary, looks like a small animal from Pets' Corner, the sort that'll take cheese and onion crisps from the palm of your hand. The stories that accrue to it all have the same punch line:

'We have a prison but it's only been used twice in a hundred years. A girl was put there for stealing some clothes but she complained of being shut up so the door was left open so that her friends could sit and talk to her.' (FRANCIS DILLON, BBC Radio documentary, 1938)

'I think my father got his ideas for the prison scene in *Mr. Pye* from the prison on Sark. There was a terrible drunk who fell madly in love with a woman who refused him. He put a bomb outside her front door. He was caught. . . . I don't think the bomb went off . . . he went to Guernsey but he came back to Sark prison and left the same evening when it was dark, they forgot to lock the door.' (SEBASTIAN PEAKE)

The weather improves visibly, that is the mist lifts, as we troop on, past the school – 'Just mind the bikes as we go round this dangerous corner' – down past La Manoir to the Dixcart Valley discussing the rights of tenement holders – 'they can still be called upon in an emergency to find a man with a musket, although I don't think they've got muskets any more. . . . Have we any bird watchers today, any bird people? Any interested people in birds?' Everyone looks towards the tandems for a lead but they have chosen lichen for their special subject and just look smug. 'The migrating species are all coming through now, you see masses of different things, goldfinches, greenfinches, wagtails, some have gone already . . . what natural fauna have we got, fauna? Oh squirrels, no foxes, no, nothing like that. Hundreds of rabbits, we have now got hedgehogs, Seigneur's wife brought them in, a bit of a controversy about that, they eat slugs. We've got thousands of frogs that eat slugs as well but we're not sure how the chain is going to work but we'll see. Not decided by committee, no. The Seigneur's wife wanted hedgehogs. Snakes? No. Ghosts? Meant to be. . . .

'Back there's an opening to a tunnel you can't see. I have been in it but you can't go in it now because it's all fallen in. It was all hewn out by slave workers during the war, they did have political prisoners here. . . . Oh wait a minute, watch your back, it's a nightmare, they're so dangerous these bikes . . . I'll show you an opening to one of these tunnels. The Germans occupied this hotel and Dixcart and they made tunnels. What they did in them I don't know. They have their own washing unit at this hotel, like a little launderette, this hotel is a good place, open all hours for a snack.'

'This is where I had coffee with Derek Jacobi,' confides a flag-planter. 'Dear Derek. We went on a walk of areas used in the film of *Mr. Pye* and he happened to be visiting the island again. We've been coming here for fifteen years, this is our granddaughter, we thought the walk would be an introduction for her. Changed? Oh, quite a bit. Quite a bit of building but the atmosphere hasn't changed.'

'Some of you may have read Mrs Tremayne's Diary, a book that came out, it was about the war years. That's the house in the book, owned by an Englishman, I believe it's up for sale. I don't know how much but don't bother. Has a heated swimming pool, you can see the solar panels through there. The swimming pool's in an enormous greenhouse . . . oh, the houses go for well over a hundred thousand something odd. The Barracks, which is not even a tenement but a leasehold, I was told over seven hundred thousand. Rumour that Paul McCartney came to see it. We would quite like it. I would. He has massive security so it's quite a good place. I was up in Kintyre where he lived and a big wall all round, I thought, poor chap. . . . I like his music, the Kintyre music that he did, beautiful, made me go there. Oh the grape vine, rumours, you stand up here and it would be totally different down there . . . journalists all the time, from all over the world, through the summer months. They don't come and see us in the winter, it's too rough. There's an old-fashioned drain there. . . . There is a lot of interest in it, the island, because we are, I suppose, the last of the little feudal islands or places, whether we can keep it up I don't know. . . .'

Across the road to the Coupée and Little Sark, up the track to Beauregard – 'Nice view here of the choppy sea' – by chance we meet the lecturer on sea anemones sitting on the grass, tandems smile knowingly, then on to the subject of dogs.

'We say this rather delicately now, the Seigneur is allowed to keep a lady dog, because if you say the Seigneur is allowed to keep a bitch . . . I've heard one or two funny remarks. And doves. The poor dogs get very upset, even with the spayed bitches. You know we had one lady who came with about four or five poodles, she came for a fortnight, stayed in self-catering, and one of these poodles came into season. Well, there wasn't a dog to be seen, this whole house ringed by dogs, how they ever got off the island I don't know.

'We've got a local man who's a radio ham, his big mast got blown away in the hurricane, he has got a telescopic one now. He can reach Russia and the Falklands, all over the place, we knew what was going on in the Falklands. Now I think we're going to have a little shower, it won't be much, we'll get down under the hedge . . . it's bound to go over . . . sensible people with flat shoes and raincoats, people I've had, stilettos, we do get some. . . . That little house in front, we had a very high wind one year and the whole lot went up at night. One lady in there and all the men on the island heard of the emergency so they put ropes over the house and hung onto it. They got her out and they saved the house, clinging on, well, all night really. That house nearly disappeared, you can tell the type of winds we have here in the winter.'

Finally a look at the washing line at Beauregard, 'The longest line in the west. The story is that the actor Denis Price used to come and talk to the lady who owns this washing line. She'd get to the bottom of her washing basket, she had all her little tiddy bits, you know, she wanted to hang on the line, undies and things, and Denis would still be talking, probably didn't notice. . . .'

Summertime in the arms of Juliet. Sark registers on the brain in fleeting glimpses caught from the corner of your eye. You find it in a kitchen, in a chance conversation on the road. After an awful day it creeps up and surprises you at night. It comes when, after two or three weeks, a friend comes over bringing news from home and unexpectedly you don't want to hear it. You don't want to hear it – your vehemence takes you aback. You want to put your hands over your ears, or shut the mouth that's telling you. This is how far the tide has taken you, how much you have shed without knowing it, how little you regret.

> The first rhythm that they became used to was the slow
> swing from dawn to quick dusk. They accepted the
> pleasures of morning, the bright sun, the whelming sea
> and sweet air, as a time when play was good and life so
> full that hope was not necessary and therefore forgotten.
> (WILLIAM GOLDING, *Lord of the Flies*)

Nothing is quite enough. Talk sponge cakes, eat blackberries, wait whilst the farmer beds a calf . . . the centenary of T. S. Eliot (who's Sartre?) can't compare to being a quiet white stone settled softly in Sark mud.

You haven't sent a postcard and the letters sent from home are skimmed and cast aside: 'The bypass has started, bunting marks the carriageways. When they cut the trees down (you remember that line of trees?) they fell as we fall in dreams, flat on their faces, hands bound behind their backs. Then sometime after the fall the shower of their leaves. They've put the fence posts up now, crows already line the route, waiting for something to get run over. They're building a mound in front of your house, at first we thought it was a layby but we're told it is a mound. Your house in the country is in a road sandwich but a mound makes it one and a half roads really, a mound makes it less than two.'

You think of the yachtsmen who fracture the night peace, who get drunk at Beauregard and raise hell as they reel down the lane past the old man's house to Havre Gosselin. How you raved at the yachtsmen who shout at sea and on land and yet yachtsmen at the bottom of the garden seem like fairies now; you'd rather watch yachtsmen than count containerway lorries, Marks and Spencer's Fashion Flow. . . .

For weeks you haven't read a paper, cared a hoot, the only point of Radio Guernsey with its heavenly choir to announce news and weather forecast is to gloat. 'Floods in the area of St Peter Port, congestion, adverse weather conditions, indefinite delays at the airport, papers stuck in Jersey, postal strike, green house pest, egg scare, temporary road signs. . . .'

God is Deafe, the weather rages, the ozone layer is shot. . . . A child brings news of the duckpond: 'When I just started off I hit the bank, I had to pedal downhill, standing up, couldn't freewheel because of the wind. Every time you came to a gap in the hedge the wind and rain blew at you and made you go into the middle of the road. Ducks were all in the road, loads of them, I went round the corner and almost ran them over, all up on the bank and in the middle of the road. They all crossed in a line, I had to do an emergency stop because of the ducks. The pond was a bit deeper than usual and it came out a bit more as well.'

No news except the sea mist rolling in, eclipsing first Guernsey, then Brechou, then the monument, then the field, creeping in the windows in the early morning, the typing paper so sodden that it can't be rolled into the carriage. God is Deafe, make do and mend, after an unbecoming struggle Crusoe has now repaired the typewriter – hurled at one or other airport – by weighting down the plastic casing, grey and loathsome casing, with string and stones. 'What have you done to the typewriter, are you frightened that it's going to blow away?' No one is frightened of anything. With nothing more pressing on the agenda we wonder where the butterflies, which skim the field in sunshine, disappear to in the mist and wind and rain?

How the wind blows, how the sea rages. The old man has gone away and apart from a niece who comes in to stoke the stove we are left to guard the house. Meticulously tidy now, uncharacteristically organised: collect the water, boil the blackberries, wash the saucepan, wring out the cloth; playing house. Shut the doors, close the windows, turn the lights out and worry, 'something's banging', in the windy darkness.

How quickly the summer life is replaced by the winter one, socks and jumpers on the pulley above the stove, whisky with Mrs Bealie Reynolds and your feet in an extra jumper tucked onto the hard horsehair sofa in the room with the piano. And then, how suddenly the weather changes on an island, out to the line by the sheds and the ash buckets with the old man's peg basket once again.

Mrs Bealie Reynolds now holds the broken sash window open,

sun streaming through at the end of the afternoon. Autumn on its way now, watching the starlings swoop in close formation, congregate, 'strange fruit', like plums on the pine tree. Leaves on the path edged with Ormer shells in concrete, hydrangeas bounce like breasts after a squall of wind and rain. Typing in the empty dining room, looking out across the Gouliot passage, watching a bird until it flies out of sight beyond the flaking frame.

# 12

# Feudalism and the Finance Industry

William next invented a system according to which everybody had to belong to somebody else, and everybody else to the King. This was called the Feutile System, and in order to prove that it was true he wrote a book called the Doomsday Book, which contained an inventory of all the Possessions of all his subjects; after reading the book through carefully William agreed with it and signed it, indicating to everybody that the Possessions in it were now his.

(W. C. SELLAR AND R. J. YEATMAN, *1066 And All That*)

Mary Balsen's *The Story of the Nations – Medieval England*, published in 1903, is the nearest I have come to the book from which we learnt feudalism at our convent school. Feudalism aged ten or eleven meant colouring. Our exercise books were lined on the left, blank on the right and if you made a mess of either page it was hard to get the book back into synch without revealing how much had been torn out. Whilst it was difficult in geography to put coffee and rubber into a small smudged tracing of South America, feudalism, neatness itself, was made for the blank quarto page.

The manor had beehives, duck pond and dovecot. There was common land (pigs, acorn and firing), a mill, a church, cottages around a strip field system, drawn in threes with a ruler. Tidy, everyone knew who they were, 'I'm a villein, you're a cottar.' No one could leave the village on pain of death. Charity was something you gave to pilgrims in a bowl. The manorial court would meet now and then (the meeting place always visualised as a clearing in the New Forest), tithes were collected and stacked in the barn, peasants took up arms to fight, or downed tools to work, according to his lordship's whim. Feudalism was, above all, tidy. Tidy, before more astute historians began to see it as an abstract concept muddling up those neatly rulered lines. Tidy, and one can't help feeling that, when it comes to feudalism, first knowledge of it, however limited, was the best. That, give or take a Sokeman and forgetting Norfolk, feudalism was as good a means of social control as mortgages. It happened a long time ago and it worked.

If Sark markets its culture for tourists then it is its feudalism as much as its coastline that draws the punters in. Yet, without the National Trust – one would land in the shop – seigneurial oven gloves, Prévot Pots, scented peasant drawer liners – and then go on to the harbour. Without the National Trust to get the Dime Cart rolling, to get their wig department onto the forelock flick, Sark feudalism is virtually invisible. The system of land tenure, the basis of feudalism, does not exactly leap up and hit one in the eye.

One lovely evening towards the end of August Elie Vaudin and The Englishman sat half-way down the cliff, by the side of an old grey well, wherein graceful fern fronds were reflected in the velvety black water.

'Vaudin,' said Herbet, 'I am anxious to know something about land tenure in these islands. Can you give me any information?'

'It is like this, Monsieur. In these islands there are two ways of holding property; it is held as a farm, and we pay annual rents for it, and it is yet our own to go down to our children for ever, freehold property I have heard English gentlemen say it is. But about the buying of it, sir, when it first comes into families, I'll explain to you by the family of De Carteret here. He is rich, but it is the same law for the poorest fisherman! The grandfather, William de Carteret, bought some land worth twelve hundred pounds; the money was not paid at once, it was given to rent, as we say. William de Carteret was to pay in quarters – a quarter, sir, is £20. He had to pay a quarter of the price down; after that forty-five quarters a year. He paid a quarter down, Monsieur, as a sign he would work the land properly, and pay the rent regularly. If he did not attend to the property, there might be a saisie, that means that De Carteret might be turned out, and he would lose the quarter he had paid down. But as all went well, Monsieur, and the contract was passed, De Carteret could cut down trees, work and drain the land, and do what he could to make things grow. Then, Monsieur, that land goes down, under the same conditions, to his son, or to the nearest relation, if he has no children. Yes, sir, yes, you're right! It's a good plan, but there is more. Sometimes these yearly quarters are fixed – settled – such as 20s. per quarter; sometimes they alter, so as to depend upon the value of a quarter of wheat – and that's fair – that's fair, sir; for, if corn is high, the farmer can afford a high rent, and if the corn is low, he need not pay more than his crop will let him.'

(E. GALLIENNE ROBIN, *Extremes Meet: A Song of Sark*)


The Law of primogeniture is very strict; and, in case of their being no male issue, the eldest daughter inherits before the nephew. Where there is no issue at all, the property reverts to the Seigneur. His great trouble is with the younger sons; who, being portionless, must needs go forth into the world to seek their fortunes, and are afterwards desirous of returning to their native shore with their wives and families. He is obliged to prevent this or the island would be soon over-populated; and this protectionist principle is, under the circumstances, necessary enough.

(*Household Words*, 1855)


[In 1927] . . . notices were posted under her [Sibyl Hathaway's] name at the entrance to the church, giving warning that many old laws and customs which had long since lapsed into disuse were to be reintroduced. Seigneurial tithes of crops were once again to be paid in kind, rather than money . . . and the old law forbidding games of chance or

164

payment of entrance fees to any entertainment, such as whist drives and dances, was also to be re-enforced. . . . [The Sarkese attitude to the reintroduction of these restrictions] drew the attention of the international press, many of whose members made much in their reports of the woman ruler who wielded such feudal power.

(BARBARA STONEY, Sibyl, Dame of Sark)

'When they were mistaken or had misguided ideas the Dame would tell them so. I remember when some of them started selling their tenements while I was there and then grumbling in Chief Pleas meetings about not having this and not being able to do that and I can hear her saying to her people that they had to realise if they sold their tenements that they could not have their cake and eat it. She used that phrase and she would tell them when it was anything like that. She upheld her authority but she was marvellous to them, she would stop and speak to any of them. I remember her as a friend. In the days when she had her electric bathchair, she called them by their Christian names and did a lot of kindness. I was very sad when she went because it was the end of an era. It was a drop of two generation to the new Seigneur and you can't expect it to have gone along the same. The modern age, the modern person.'

Francis Dillon's 1938 radio documentary describes arrangements made for the corvée, two days' free labour on the roads or the harbour provided by the islanders for the common good. Twelve members of Chief Pleas, 'the funeral procession', walked the island to report on the condition of roads and hedges. There was no age limit to the corvée and the broadcast talks of men of eighty out there with the rest of them. Those who absented themselves paid fines which were transmuted to provide drink for the other workers.

These days the road gangs are paid by the island. In the early winter you pass them all the time, cutting back the banks, like Cornish hedges, tidying up the summer growth, smoothing out the unmade roads, covering the granite chippings from the quarry by the harbour with a fine layer of sandy grit. Road work is slow spade work, it seems impossible that they're ever going to finish; you pass them in the morning and you pass them in the same place on your way back. Passing people two or three times a morning on Sark is tough on body language. In the backwoods of Ireland even motorists hail each other by wagging a finger, all right I suppose if you have a windscreen but easily misinterpreted on a bike. 'Hello' is either caught by the wind or sounds like the start of a conversation. Pretending one's so preoccupied one hasn't seen people is silly when one has to swerve to avoid them. In the end I settled for a bow of the head; cycling through a crowd I felt like little Noddy.

Shaped stones, the size of a footstool, now used to hold down roofs of hen houses, pig sties and old sheds, or half buried in the long grass, were once apparently used as weights for feudal dues but no one I spoke to knew the detail of the when and how. There is no museum on the island and feudal relics, which must, one imagines, be kept at the Seigneurie, exist outside it only in the heads of the old Sarkese.

'The poor tax used to be paid in wheat, now it's in money. There was a pewter measure, a sittonier. I remember my father used to make a pile of wheat after he'd winnowed it. He said, "When Mr G. has passed with his cabot there won't be much left." '

Much is made in documentaries of the quaintness of the island parliament and its laws, leaning heavily on rules on rabbit catching and the rights of wreck. Chief Pleas is portrayed as a toy-town parliament with nothing nastier in the woodshed than an old character with one too many bunnies up his jumper.

'When Guernsey produces a law which is obviously of universal significance, a drugs law, anything to do with foreign policy that it is sensible to apply to Sark as well, Chief Pleas will have a copy of it and will ratify it so that it is law on Sark as well. They just take over the relevant Guernsey law. They can also, if they feel like it, refuse to take over a Guernsey law but in the case of drugs they take over what's appropriate.'

'One of the carriage drivers smuggled marijuana in and got caught. To begin with there are sniffer dogs at Guernsey. He went to a friend in England asking for more marijuana and sending him money and the friend wrote back with his address in the letter and the sniffer dogs got it at the Guernsey post office. They sent the letter on to its destination then came and arrested him and arrested the person who sent the letter. He went to prison here, they jailed him for a little while then he came back to Sark, then he left the island when he got into more trouble for another reason. He ran out of favour again and went. We've had three drugs cases this year [1988] because people don't think they're going to get caught here. One of them went to smoke his cigarette, his joint, right by the window where you could smell it, not thinking anybody here would recognise the smell. Well we recognised the smell and he got nobbled by the constable. The case was particularly bad because he'd involved a Sark youngster who in fact was frightened to bits and who will probably never get anywhere near marijuana again. I suppose Chief Pleas are a shade paranoiac about it but it's a fault in the right direction.'

But who is cleaning up the garbage in the heads of our policy-makers? Like Mrs Thatcher, our socialist cabinet is obsessed with progress and growth, which inevitably takes precedence over environmental pollution. And while huge amounts are squandered on eradicating cannabis, a much more insidious narcotic bends the minds of our movers and shakers – tourism. We are crying out to be the Mexico of Asia (our dollar already apes the peso). Sydney's skyline is being moulded into a suitable victim for pack-rape by packaged tourists, with high-rise hotels, more airports, theme parks, shopping malls and crocodile parks. Having seen many spots from Bodrum to Bali homogenised and served up in styrofoam cups, it is galling – if perhaps just – to watch tourism contaminate my own play-pen.

(RICHARD NEVILLE, *Independent Magazine*, 22 April 1989)

'I've known Chief Pleas arguing about laws when they'd have been better off down in the west bays gathering the harvest the October gales have brought in . . . it's a matter of who brings it ashore has it . . . there's usually something to get wet for.'

(FRANCIS DILLON BBC Radio documentary, 1938)

'Some of my rights are valuable, the right of wreck for one, but if a fisherman comes to the Seigneurie and tells me that he has found wine or timber or similar wreckage I usually let him keep it. In some cases I take half. If they conceal the find, and word usually gets round to me, I take it all.'
(DAME OF SARK, Francis Dillon BBC Radio documentary,
1938)

'So this man says to the Dame, "Remind me. What are the rules for flotsam and jetsam, Madame?"

"Everything above the high water mark is mine," she says.

"Madame," he replied, "go to Grand Greve and collect your whale." '

The radical change in the make-up of the island population [post 1918] was reflected in the personnel of the Quarantaine Tenants, who alone had a voice in the control of Island affairs through their vote in Chief Pleas. The ownership of these tenements had become concentrated in a relatively small number of individuals; members of the Baker family held nine tenements, the Godfray family held five, the Seigneur held three, and ten were in the hands of non-islanders; this development meant that the generality of the population was deprived of adequate representation in Chief Pleas. In an attempt to redress this imbalance the Privy Council approved on 20 June 1922 the Sark Reform Law by which twelve People's Deputies were added to the membership of Chief Pleas. These Deputies being elected by adult suffrage of the whole population, all males over the age of 20 and all females over the age of 30 being granted the right to vote.
(*Fief of Sark*)

'Some of the members of Chief Pleas never say a peep. The island is run by young men of forty, the old men are there and I think their advice is taken but the actual doing is now done by younger men. Some tenants never turn up for Chief Pleas. I think the Deputies do most of the work, fortunately they can be got rid of. They're up for election every three years, you can vote them out. People are a bit shy of putting a tenant on a committee because you can't get shot of him if he's no good, he's on that committee forever, but after three years you can vote someone out, you see. Where does power lie? I think it probably lies with the Seigneur whatever he says. He does an awful lot of work, dealing with the Guernsey people, he's the guy that actually deals with it.'

'If they pass a law they want us to ratify and they want us to do something on the same lines they can put pressure on and we usually adopt the law. Most people say that power lies with Chief Pleas and it does really but Chief Pleas manage to mismanage it. Past masters at bumbling mismanagement, that's why Sark is the way it is I'm sure, four hundred years of mismanagement makes it work.'

'At one time the church kept the island together but not any more. An English resident said to me that if the English ever took power completely she'd leave at once, this was what she'd come to get away from.'

'At the beginning you think, this and that should be done, must be done, but after ten years or so you become reactionary, that nothing must change.'

> All the nice people were poor; at least, that was a general axiom, the best of the rich being poor in spirit.
> (MURIEL SPARK, *The Girls of Slender Means*)

'It's like Sodom and Gomorrah here, no need to work. It was quite discreet when it started, now its escalated, perhaps 40 per cent are involved. It benefits the individual, it's not an industry for the island, the "trickle-down" theory is just nonsense. There's no need for initiatives, thinking of other industries apart from tourism, no need for anything if this continues.'

'The man's not born yet who can keep everybody happy. Life has become too easy, all the same problems as affect England, religion, discipline, money.'

> The series of naval wars with France during the eighteenth century continued to yield ever richer prizes to the privateers, and to afford profitable employment for the younger sons of Sark families. In the interludes of peace the imposition of excise duties on a wide range of commodities by the British Government to pay for the costs of the wars created a vast new industry of smuggling duty-free goods. The proximity of the Channel Islands to the south coast of England made them an ideal base of operations for breaking down bulk commodities into small portable packages, and the manufacture of small kegs for the transport of wines and spirits became a major occupation. This new, "fair trade", as it was euphemistically termed, made good the loss to the Island economy caused by the collapse of the cottage knitting industry which proved unable to compete with the factory machine-made products.
>
> *(Fief of Sark)*

Spring 1988. Among the travellers coming up the Harbour Hill from the 10.00 boat, a neatly suited businessman carrying a briefcase stands out from the crowd, like Superman ready for the off.

'There are some people on the island who make a living out of off-shore directorships of companies. They use their Sark addresses and sign a bit of paper and that's all there is to it. We call it "the Sark Lark" and I think they're going to put a stop to it.'

\*

'Everyone knows about the Sark Lark but not everyone knows who's in it. I know one guy who makes a living out of running companies through Sark. He sits there with his computer and his modem and he's in touch with the financial world, he processes stuff for companies.'

'I think the Sark Lark is a typical way of approaching a problem, just rake in the cash and cock-a-snoop at the others, it's definitely a Channel Island trait not a Sark trait. We'd like them to be Robin Hood but it certainly isn't like that, taking the cash and spreading it around the community to the good, I suspect it isn't actually working like that although there are obviously enormous benefits to having wealthy people around. They're employing people, if the roof needs fixing they wouldn't get up and bang it on themselves. What happens when the plug is pulled out is another matter, the plug will get pulled out one day, won't it, there's talk about it happening very soon. If they pull the plug out rapidly I can see a lot of people on the island getting a bit of a shock. Apart from screwing the tourists there is no other industry.'

'I wouldn't talk about it publicly too often. I have tried when I first came here to explain what I felt about it but I never quite could explain myself to their satisfaction, basically explaining it to people who aren't doing it which is probably the worst. They think it ought to be harder to earn money, the good old work ethic. You have to be seen to be doing it, there's nothing like hard work here for credibility. Making money from the Sark Lark is far more of a taboo here than being a child of the German Occupation or to talk about sex or death. It's quite nice to go somewhere now and again and to realise that making money is not a taboo everywhere. Is there a residual guilt from money earned easily? I wouldn't say it was easy. If it entailed a pick and a shovel I'd probably feel easier about it. I have now and again lost my temper with people who have asked me to contribute to various charity events. I like the line to be drawn to where the decision is mine rather than the decision of the person who is coming with the box. On a few occasions I have turned round to the person and asked, "Are you asking me to contribute or telling me?", there is a rather finely drawn line.'

'There are some exceptional people here, people who light up the room when they go into it. They'll give and give and tackle almost anything. The year that two of them were constables there were two nasty deaths and they'd never seen a corpse before. They were scraping people off the rocks when they'd gone off the Coupée and had to fish a body from the sea that had been in the sea for a couple of months, that sort of thing. They did it because it's got to be done, they do it. Their ingenuity . . . when the *Mr. Pye* was filmed they turned themselves into a complete production department and the ex-lighthouse keeper was a graphic artist, he can paint anything. They did an awful lot because they enjoyed doing it. Sark people don't think of money because they enjoy what they're doing, they don't worry about it.'

> The introduction of money into a community which
> previously had not known what money was, did great
> harm and converted the St. Kildans into what George
> Seton called, 'the most knowingest people I have ever
> come across.'
> (TOM STEEL, *The Life and Death of St Kilda*)

> So many other values have diminished: patriotism,
> religion, family. All that's really left is money. It's the way
> you keep the score. It's one of the few values that still
> survives.
> (STUDS TERKEL, *The Great Divide*)

'It's just human nature, isn't it, money is more corrosive than sea salt. It undoubtedly makes a difference whether your face fits, whether you're considered to belong to the island. Honest toil? Some of the financiers will never be accepted as a local on the basis of what they do, as far as we're concerned they don't do anything. Because he doesn't do honest toil he hasn't got a hope. We worship money. We certainly judge people, pub-type people, we would judge them probably to their detriment if we knew they were making a lot of money from the Sark Lark. It's not a question of using Sark's name but about people having money for doing nothing. A great many people are in it.'

'Somewhere along the line there were people, people from England, came here and retired, they had a knowledge of the finance industry and they were the ones who were approached. I think that has changed, there are Sarkese involved in it, once you're in. . . . It makes the headlines because it's all to do with credibility. England has begun to look at tax havens all around and there's a desire to be as respectable as possible. There's the laundering of money, all these things cropping up, you always hear of the bad ones. Guernsey and Jersey and the other tax havens are trying to make their things as respectable as possible and the pressure from the UK being aware of what's happening on the Channel Islands. I think the Channel Islands have decided to clean up their act and as an act of good faith I think they're leaning towards Sark as the less credible financial centre, to an outside view they are the weak part of the chain. Sark gets the short end of the stick because it is easily criticisable by centres of expertise like Guernsey, but I think it's just a continuation of what the Channel Islands have always done. The actual purchase of the Seigneurie was through privateering profits. How old does new money have to get?'

A notable feature of Sark life throughout the 18th Century was the building of new and larger houses; this expenditure was the direct result of the new prosperity that was enjoyed by many of the Tenants from the profits of privateering. In this activity the Slowley family were particularly prominent. Le Grand Beauregard, the chief family tenement, where the Tenant was Robert Slowley, a nephew of the privateer Captain at Jaspellerie, was rebuilt in 1736; two other houses, la Ville Farm and la Moinerie, where the Tenants were married to Slowley wives, were rebuilt before 1730.

(*Fief of Sark*)

'When you talk to other directors in Guernsey or Jersey, whoever's slightly in the know about the impending law, say, "What are you going to do?" and some say, "Well, we don't really know yet," so it could be the end. At the moment it isn't and I think they'll probably find some other ship to sink. At the end of the day it's the individual's choice, whoever owns this money if he chooses to employ me. . . .'

'And these off-shore invaders should be penalised. I'd like them to be well and truly taxed. I still think it's very short-sighted that way of introducing money to the island because there's quite a few over here, they will suffer. They've risen their way of life and they'll be dropped right back. You never miss what you've never had.'

> End of 'Sark Lark' will hit islanders.
> Everyone in Sark will be affected indirectly by the loss of offshore Guernsey company directorships, said Sark deputy Raymond Gibson on a BBC news bulletin yesterday.
> He pointed out in his interview with BBC financial correspondent James Long that although only 50 people may be acting as company directors, indirectly everyone in the island will feel the effects of the drop in income.
> James Long asked Mr. Gibson why Guernsey would want to cream off Sark's business. Mr. Gibson said that he had been told that Guernsey would make more money by doing so.
> The BBC were presenting a cameo view of the tax haven status of Guernsey and Sark, and intimated that an ill wind may be blowing through the island, causing it to abandon tax loopholes such as the 'Sark Lark'.
> Mr. Long said that Guernsey was defending its position that it was not a home for hot money.
> (*Guernsey Evening Press and Star*, November 1988)

I want to hear the Sark women gossiping in Norman-French patois, I want to ride up Harbour-Hill with Alfred or Philip or Henry. There are brown old men there

waiting to tell me of the Sark of their simple childhood and
how little it has changed.

(LEONARD CLARK, *Island of 100 Bays*)

So this is a real old-fashioned briefcase. . . .

'I think Sark doesn't work in quite a few respects. We're awfully
poor. The island exchequer is desperately poor compared to what
Guernsey's reaping out of its tourist and finance industry because
here the individuals are doing it not the island. I think the
individuals make the money and the island doesn't. The island
gets only the landing tax and the booze and there is a local tax to
provide for the old people which is a pittance really.'

'The one thing that Sark does have is scale. I'm sure that in any
family, village, country, scale is one of the most important
determinants. I believe that quite a lot of studies have been done
by economists and sociologists and people trying to think about
how society organises itself on the issue of scale and I would have
thought that Sark has it theoretically all ways. They can really get
something going to their own advantage. They can have a lot of
the advantages that the twentieth century has brought without so
many of the disadvantages, they're in a position to do that in
principle. In practice there just isn't the experience, foresight
amongst the people living there for them to be able to realise that
potential but I'm sure that the worst won't happen because it's a
manageable scale.'

The other day I met a friend who told me that on the hill
above the prison there are numerous chalets and
bungalows. I can hardly imagine it. It is selfish to want to
deny the other people beauty that one has known but I
feel I dare never go back.

(EVE ORME, *Sark Remembered*)

'The English have the money to buy the good houses and they
destroy them if they possibly can and the island has no teeth in its
legislation to prevent that sort of thing. Chalet building, all those

175

things, Chief Pleas can't do anything when they're up against someone clever, ruthless. One man who put up some chalets, he said, "I'm taking you on. I know the rules, you don't. The rules of what I can or can't do," that's what he said and he went ahead and built them.'

> The structural change from agriculture to tourism also creates changes in land use patterns. Tourism increases the competition for land, raising land prices and encouraging sales, contributing to the fragmentation of landholdings. Land is sold in smaller units and at higher prices and this contributes to inflation. The victims of this inflation are the young residents trying to purchase land or homes.
> (EMANUEL DE KADT, *Tourism: Passport to Development?*)

'Any more building will spoil Sark. A lot of houses, they're for people in commerce and again a lot of families are split up and they all want, like the youngsters on the mainland, they all want their flat so they build themselves a house. If they separate and pick up with somebody different, there's two houses gone for the same couple. I can think of half a dozen off-hand without mentioning any names. It's the twentieth century again. Absentee landlords should be fined at least £100 for each meeting of Chief Pleas they don't attend, £300 at least.'

> Fortunately there is no unemployment in Sark. We have no trade unions. Every man can turn his hand to any trade that comes his way – it may be building, farming, fishing, carpentry or general trading. However it must be admitted that the island relies for its great prosperity on the ever-increasing number of summer visitors and day tourists. During the last few years these have averaged some 28,000 per annum. Perhaps we are now beginning to rely too much on this import trade and are tempted to neglect our farming and fishing, but for which we would have starved during the German Occupation.
> (DAME OF SARK, *Autobiography*)

Changes in patterns of agricultural production in many
rural economies are not endemic to tourists. Many of the
changes have been the result of demographic pressures,
technical progress, employment opportunities, outside of
the rural economy and modification in patterns of land
ownership. Tourism, though not always a major cause, has
often contributed to the acceleration of such changes . . .
many farmers have left the land to pursue more lucrative
jobs in the tourist industry.
(EMANUEL DE KADT, *Tourism: Passport to Development?*)

Arguments were still taking place over the new deep-water
harbour, the construction of which, by the spring of 1938,
was about to start after numerous suggestions and plans had
been rejected by Chief Pleas. . . . A *Sunday Dispatch* article in
June put forward other reasons for disquiet. Headed 'Sark is
scared', it reported that some residents thought the new
scheme would not just bring revenue to the island. A bigger
harbour would mean, they thought, 'bigger boats and
cheaper people – the tripper – and Sark had always tried to
avoid this type of visitor'. The islanders, according to the
article, foresaw an unwanted change and the regular visitors
were also objecting. . . . Sibyl scoffed at what she termed this
'romantic nonsense' but the wrangling continued and, as so
often happened, she became the scapegoat for much of the
dissatisfaction.
(BARBARA STONEY, *Sibyl, Dame of Sark*)

I have spent my life attempting to do two things. I have
attempted to hold together a harassed and a confused people
by trying to keep them in touch with the life they knew before
they were overrun. It wasn't a life of material ease but it had
its assurances and it had its dignity. And I have done that by
acknowledging and indeed honouring the rituals and
ceremonies and beliefs these people have practised since
before history, long before the God of Christianity was ever
heard of. And at the same time I have tried to open these
people to the strange new ways of Europe, to ease them into
the new assessment of things, to nudge them towards

177

changing evaluations and beliefs. Two pursuits that can scarcely be followed simultaneously. Two tasks that are almost self-cancelling. But they have got to be attempted because the formation of nations and civilizations is a willed act, not a product of fate or accident.

(BRIAN FRIEL, *Making History*)

'The price you pay for tourism is just too big. If they want to cater for tourists they've got to decide, they never really have, as to what they're catering for. They've gone for the really lowest common denominator. Sark could have represented quite a beautiful place and people went to see it as well as the coast.'

The level of irritation arising from contacts between hosts and tourists will be determined by the mutual compatibility of each, with the assumption that even with seemingly compatible groups, sheer numbers may generate tensions.

(EMANUEL DE KADT, *Tourism: Passport to Development?*)

'They put pressure on us in Guernsey to run an extra bus from the harbour, that's just an example of the pressure they put on. Then they'll say about the carriages that they want to fix it, shorten the carriage ride so it all fits nicely. . . . A whole heap of little things like that are changing the way we do things. We're out to grab the cash that's for sure, but I'm not sure if we still call the tune.'

Tourism is now such big business that by 2000 it will be the largest industry in the world. As tour operators vie to find previously 'hidden' destinations, travellers lament the discovery of their favourite spots. But do tourists bring any long-term benefits to the countries they descend upon, or do they simply create new problems and resentments? . . . Professor Brian Archer, head of the University of Surrey's tourist management studies department, argued that although not all countries benefited from tourism, in many cases it could act as a catalyst for development.

The industry encouraged the building of roads and

airports, it provided a market for local farmers and craft workers and brought in revenue for governments. Even those not directly involved in tourism benefited from the money spent by tourists working its way through a country's economy.

(London Conference on Tourism, 1988)

'. . . this difference between what it's actually like living on Sark and this view people have of the tranquil coastal scenery, gentle little fishermen. . . . You can see why it seems like that because we're all tucked up here on top of the island. We're in a hopeless paradox in Sark, aren't we, stuck on the horns of a dilemma here. Never mind the finance industry, tourism on its own is at a sort of stage where we're not really getting the benefits at all. Tourism is beginning to cost more than it's actually worth, cost to the whole fabric of society. We're being asked to change our way of operations to suit the tourist now.'

'Sark was put on the map too much in a way I suppose. You see the visitors that went to Sark in the fifties and early sixties were the type of people who went there year after year, just to walk, to love and delight in the beauty of the naturalness of Sark. Somewhere utterly and completely different. You breathed a different air and you felt a different atmosphere where everything was really at peace except for the wildness of the weather.'

'We've got enough tourists, we don't need any more and if they introduce any more to the island it won't be good. I think it's partly why people come here, for peace and quiet and because it's not touristy. Tourists, they've all got blinkers on.'

'We should get rid of the English residents and go back to running Sark ourselves. I'd like to see more tourists and no residents. A hundred thousand tourists a year wouldn't bother me.'

'Of course the community does generate sufficient amount itself to keep healthy but not at this population level. I mean you don't

179

need industry to get by do you, Mrs Thatcher's proving that. If the island suddenly got polluted then tourism would go, it's a troubling thought. I'm sure we'd get by, but what would happen? We do have, for example, a pollution problem on the island without mains drains, if the water supply of a major hotel, for example, got polluted from somebody else's sewage – the water of course on this island is something else! – and if it got out that someone had been poisoned you can just imagine the BBC holiday programme, but would it stop people coming? The thing about a decline in agriculture is that as soon as people get hungry they're back out there digging like fury aren't they?'

'It makes me wonder how long it's going to work. There are so many things that could happen, it's a fragile thing to base things on. It would only take somebody to come over with some sort of infection or other . . . an infection on the island or an oil slick and then what would the island do? I mean you could say now that it is absolutely dependent on tourists.'

> Sometimes spirited discussions take place in the Chief Pleas, and Bob was delighted by a story I told him of an incident which occurred when my father was Seigneur. A very old, deaf member fell asleep while the meeting was discussing a landing tax of sixpence a head on all tourists and woke up later when the debate was about a bounty for exterminating rats. He was just in time to hear one of the members say that he objected to poison being put down on the land, whereupon he leaped to his feet, still dreaming of tourists, and exclaimed: 'I quite agree with the speaker. I know that they leave gates open and go through the crops, but to use poison is going too far.'
> (DAME OF SARK, *Autobiography*)

# 13

## Countries of the Mind

I am not sure whether Sark is a place at all or simply exists as contrast. Sark appears on the horizon when you're stuck on a London railway station on a winter night, you've left someone else's coat in a crypt in Battersea, and Casey Jones, a burger bar, is the only place that's warm.

No smoking. You perch on a plastic chair; a looped tape plays the James Bond theme, 'Nobody does it better'; a handful of drunks; some mutilated pigeons; above your head cardboard pictures of burgers swing in the wind. Deathly blandness, cold in the soul and up Sark comes like a dolphin playing.

The train, not knee deep in litter, not awash with urine, just deeply ingrained, the upholstery, the floor, the ashtrays, ingrained with years of dirt. Slump in a corner, look into the darkness, the train sweeps past the place you left the coat. Across the aisle a huge man, rowing blue, unlaces a pair of shoes which – for this is England – establish him without question as a jolly decent chap. A tarty girl with a plastic bag observes him. 'Can I trouble you for a light?' Swan Vestas matches passed across. She lights a cigarette and takes a book from the plastic bag, it's Salman Rushdie's *Satanic Verses* and she is already half way through it.

You haven't got a paper or a book. You think of other headlines, other journeys, of the train to St Austell, when a young Irishman who, for reasons unexplained, travels weekly to Cornwall to deposit money, tells you about a friend who was knifed when he went to a lock-up garage in south London to collect some speakers for his stereo. He died on the street on a weekday morning.

'Can you look at the prison and see what they would have nicknamed it . . . look at the shape of it?'

Sark. You break off from typing a snippet on the collection of seaweed – someone you met in a pub remembers a Channel Island stamp, circa 1948, which depicted the collection of vraic – to curse some idiot mother who, while you were working, has fed your ten-year-old with a video film that would shake the sensibility of Vlad the Impaler. A friend walks round a London park with her eyes closed imagining she's somewhere else. . . .

London, Sark, places distorted by the stereotypes we're happy with, the ones that reassure us. The London cab driver and the Sark fisherman, v-signs from one, a welcoming wave from the other.

'On the country has gathered the idea of a natural way of life: of peace, innocence, and simple virtue. . . .'

Yesterday was always better, we look backward much more than we look forward. *The Country Diary of an Edwardian Lady* sells more copies than any science fiction. The extended family, roots, herbal medicine, natural childbirth, real beer, hand-thrown pots, are more attractive to us than genetic engineering and video dog. The country diary, country living, country twee, exists, blooms on, puts out new and ever stronger shoots, simultaneously with the intellectual preoccupation of exploding the myth of pastoral. We are incorrigibly plural.

> The pastoral vision is, at base, a false vision, positing a simplistic, unhistorical relationship between the ruling landowning class . . . and the workers of the land; as such its function is to mystify and to obscure the harshness of actual social and economic organization.
> (*The Penguin Book of Pastoral English Verse*)

Now this sociological filleting of the convention is a bracing corrective to an over-literary savouring of it as a matter of classical imitation and allusion, but it nevertheless entails a certain attenuation of response, so that consideration of the selected poems as made things, as self-delighting buds on the old bough of a tradition is much curtailed. The Marxist broom sweeps the poetic enterprise clean of those somewhat hedonistic impulses towards the satisfaction of aural and formal play out of which poems arise, whether they aspire to delineate or to obfuscate 'things as they are'.

(SEAMUS HEANEY, *Times Literary Supplement*, 1975)

Scrape off the sepia, get to the truth, not just the truth, the real truth, get that broom into the corners, but . . . this mission, this single-minded tunnelling which doggedly, dutifully, disturbs the hallowed ground of the way we like to think things were, can shed a different kind of darkness not more light. Out goes the arrow and skewers truth, and what a squirming one-dimensional thing it is. Like seaweed brought to the surface, it is colourless, static and dull; worst of all it's disappointing.

Place as we imagine it when we are far away cannot be trusted because we've stacked our emotional luggage in its hall. We need a little colour in our lives, we crave a little fiction, and countries of the mind exist, persist, in the realm of feelings not of facts.

There is a time when the 'Marxist broom' grows legs and stalks off back to its place in the cupboard. When Sark appears on the horizon as you cross the Great Russel from St Peter Port, no amount of knowledge about what it's really like to live there, no amount of truth, can inoculate you from its awesome pull, from something that lodges in the heart rather than the head. And nowhere on Sark is the feeling more manifest than on the 'Ile aux Chèvres', Little Sark.

On a calm day in a south-west wind, a rolling Atlantic swell sweeps over to strike Little Sark. It comes in long smooth, glassy rollers thirty to forty foot high from trough to crest and it hits the cliffs at Pierre de Buerre with a roar like all the guns of Queen Elizabeth firing at once. You can lie in your bed two miles away from the cliff and hear the seas pounding away at Little Sark.

(FRANCIS DILLON, BBC Radio documentary, 1938)

'Oh, it's different. I've said a hundred and one times I wouldn't live on Little Sark if you paid me. Well it's not so bad now that they have tractors but when it was just a bicycle, imagine, in the middle of winter on a cold day having to turn out to fetch your groceries. Too far away that Coupée, it would put me off. Beautiful bays, the Pot Bay and all round there, but I wouldn't want to live there. I can never understand. I tell them jokingly sometimes, "Oh, you're back from the wilds are you?" Very, very few live out there.'

'Little Sark was always different, you crossed the Coupée and went almost to another island, in a sense it was its own kingdom.'

> The Coupée, a narrow edge of rock several hundred feet
> in height, is the only road between Great and Little Sark;
> and, I doubt not, will one day come down with a run, and
> leave them two separate islands. The width of the summit
> is from five to eight feet, and there is no protection on
> either side. Yet I saw a native gallop at full speed on it on
> horseback.
>
> (*Household Words*, 1885)

'Special rules have always applied here, it's a very special place. The weather hasn't cut us off, the only time we were cut off in a sense was during the Occupation. We were here for quite a while and then the Germans decided after the raids – that upset them so much – so they had a guard at La Coupée and they wouldn't let us stay down here so we used to have to leave here at seven o'clock in the evening and come back at eight o'clock the next morning. Then there were more raids and it put it in their heads that we could come down here in the morning, do our work and get back to La Coupée. La Coupée was the thing . . . eleven o'clock we would go back and we'd leave all our cattle down here of course and then in the afternoon we had to get back to La Coupée at five and come down and do our work and back then at seven so we had less than four hours actually working because we had to be at La Coupée at the time they said and that went on for seven months. We had a cottage at Le Dos d'Ane and we used to stay there and make up our beds, come back and do our work, and just hope for the best that everything would be all right the next day. They had the Coupée heavily mined underneath so if the commandos landed on Little Sark they'd blow it.'

'I don't really have any connection with Little Sark. I had a friend who was over there, there's nothing to go for apart from a walk or a Sunday outing or for dinner to the Sablonnerie. There's not really anything else, there's no shops.'

'I feel if you leave here and you go to the village to do something you've done something, you've been to the village, you've done some shopping or you've seen some people you haven't seen for weeks, you come back here and you've actually done something. If you're living in the village I mean, what are you going to do? You're not going to come to Little Sark unless you've got anything to come for. I don't go to Big Sark much, three or four times perhaps in one week and then I might not go up there for months, that's how it works. Before we had the freezer, well, we had the meat safe and being the farm you'd always have things, pork and salted pork, that sort of thing, fish. There is always someone going up the village either for cargo . . . whoever would go would bring whatever. It might be you one week, it might be somebody else the next week. Everyone from here wouldn't go up because they want to do shopping, we'd make a point of "What's your order?" and one would go.'

'I think Little Sark is different. We're further afield, we don't get the same amount of trippers as Big Sark. We will get people down here at the height of the day, a lot of people, but, give or take four o'clock and everybody's gone again. We don't get them here so early, we don't have people all day like they do in the village. Furthermore a lot of people come and get to La Coupée and that's their lot so we never get the crowds down here they suffer with in the village. If I had to leave Little Sark then I'd want to leave Sark, honestly. This is home, this is where I've worked, we've got the farm, it isn't only tourism, there's always the farm that goes on once the visitors go.'

'When I was born I was the first child on Little Sark since my mother had been born there. I had cousins who took great care of me and relations who used to take me to lunch.'

'There are children on Little Sark, their mum cycles over with them for school. Old people live mainly round there. Little Sark is absolutely fantastic, it's completely different, it's sort of like . . . Sark's quite behind Guernsey but Little Sark's even more behind Big Sark isn't it? There's not new houses, sort of four-hundred-year-old cottages is the newest place built.'

Appointments arranged in England to see people on Little Sark – 'Seven o'clock. That's fine' – don't translate. Sark the feudal gem, tiny island no longer than a runway, looks and feels a lot different in the cold and the pitch black of a November night. Off in the dark on the boy's bike with the hand lamp, cycling into absolute black. The field hedges that look like one long herbaceous border of wild flowers in May loom up in the wobbling light of the lamp. A gap in the hedge and the wind hits the bicycle square on.

'I always have loved the wind. If I've been dressed for the wind I would go out and I would go in the wind anywhere. Weather didn't matter but I did become very apprehensive of the wind. We were appallingly exposed to the north-west winds, the strongest on Sark, and when I tell you that when we had a north-west gale the glass in our windows bowed in and out and . . . I have a lovely transistor and if I turned that on full blast and put it against my ear, I couldn't hear a sound. That would go on for days. It would whip great plants or shrubs out of our garden and we never saw them again. Autumn, I remember October and November particularly. The men were always desperately anxious about their boats.'

It's a long undulating road to the Coupée. A few houses off the track at Dos d'Ane, then nothing until the stone block of Plaisance Farm on the left. You hear the sea before you reach the concrete path with railings which joins Big and Little Sark, down a short steep hill and you're on it with sea hundreds of feet below on both sides. Complete darkness and exposure, gingerly pushing the bike, one hand grips the handlebars, the other holds the lamp, and the accompanying feeling, amplified by the darkness and the height, of wanting to throw yourself down.

Beyond the Coupée the road drops down gradually, more hedges looming, to a cluster of houses around an open court and a door wide open, a square of light. Inside the head of the family is watching television news, armistice, child abuse. . . . A glass of milk and talk that is difficult at first then warms up considerably, more members of the family coming into the little room, relations from other houses in the cluster, argument among the generations filling the room now, three to a sofa.

I don't say I dread the journey back, I feel I ought to be intrepid, but the head of the family, a farmer in his seventies, brings his tractor round to the door, swings my bike onto the trailer, wouldn't hear of me going back alone. We share the seat of the tractor, the bike bounces behind us, I never want to see it again or the wretched lamp. Back across the Coupée and I light the cigarette I've needed for about three hours and my host on the tractor seat has one too. We drive without meeting anything or anyone underneath the stars:

> 'Astronomy is art and philosophy as well as science,' says Crawford. 'Street lighting takes that away: it removes our sensitivity to the Universe.' Another US astronomer, Woody Sullivan, adds: 'At a time when mankind desperately needs a regular nightly vision, we have wrapped the earth in a fog.' If light pollution continues unchecked, Crawford foresees a gloomy vision of the twenty-first century. 'Future generations,' he warns, 'may never see the Universe live.'
> (International Dark Sky Association)

Hospitality, absolute peace, outside in the winter night the sound of the sea; driven all the way home and put down in safety, transported from one world to another.

*

'The documentary makers take plenty of film but they never show any of it. They show about two seconds, we pick out who's in it, and that's about all. The church – the graveyard's quite nice in summer – I wouldn't take the Avenue, that's just too unlike Sark should be. I'd go to Little Sark, talk to the old people out there.'

'I left Big Sark because I could see how it was going, way back in 1938. I wanted to capture Little Sark and keep it as I remember Big Sark when I was a kid, and it won't change, not in our lifetime.'

# 14

## *The Unbreakable Thread*

Born in Sark: bred in Sark: she was nevertheless more on than of the island. Something rebellious moved her to do the opposite: to always do the opposite. And yet, paradoxically, it was she, whenever anything derogatory was said of her home or her relations – (for her relations were everyone's relations, and everyone's relations were hers) – it was she who could be so particularly violent: she had left her tooth-marks in a tea broker's wrist, and the weals had lasted him for his entire holiday.

(MERVYN PEAKE, *Mr. Pye*)

Isolation has a good memory, and an island is an isolation. Hence the retentiveness of the islanders' recollections. There are endless traditions. It is impossible to break this thread which stretches out of sight into the night. They remember everything, a ship passing by, a hail-storm, a fish that was caught; all the more they remember their forebears. Islands are the homes of genealogies.

(VICTOR HUGO, *L'Archipel de la Manche*)

Several Sark books refer to les veilles, the watches, get-togethers at particular times of the year when people would gather in one house or another to save light and fires, knit, play games and gossip. Television has had a positively uplifting effect on such humble things as knitting, cribbage and clock patience, being able to set a video to record television soap operas or hack into a computer hasn't yet the same ring to it as attendance at a candle-lit quilting party which ends in a knees-up or the lusty singing of a glee.

'There used to be more dancing, the dance of the hats. Not many people know the tune played on the box. And the broom dance to the tune of "Cat's got the measles, the measles, the measles . . .". Two days before Christmas was La Longue Veille. Then La Serveille was the night before Christmas. We don't really do it now but we still use the term. We used to visit one another, stay up late.'

> The Seigneur is compelled to have always forty men in Sark capable of bearing arms, although he has upwards of a hundred; the whole population of the place being more than seven hundred. These men are the best shots in the Channel Islands, and are provided even with two good six-pounders. They had a field-day lately; and, after excellent practice at White Rocks, with the guns and a long range, they feigned two Russian men-of-war's boats and picked the supposed invaders off, with their muskets, very creditably. They constantly fire volleys into the caverns, to bring down any overhanging rocks, which else would fall at less expected times and destroy the boats that harbour under them. The loading of some of their private weapons for this purpose terrified us not a little. The stock was fastened to the breech by twine; so that it must have been rather hard to take the sight; and first they put the percussion-cap on, and then they loaded the gun. The spring of the lock being also broken, an urchin stood behind with a stone, to hit the hammer down when aim had been taken by the chief performer. I doubt not, however, besides the standing army of Sark, that a more effective guerilla force exists to make invasion extremely hazardous.
>
> (*Household Words*, 1855)

'Christmas Day and New Year's Day there was shooting. At the Mermaid, clay pipe. They had tickets I remember for wine or spirits and when the Pavilion was still going you shot for a turkey.

It was 3*d*. a ticket. If it was going on too long then you'd toss for first shot. There were two shoots, one at La Carrefour at 9 a.m. before divine service.'

'Shooting, oh yes! With twelve-bores, they still have it now, it's with clay pigeons, it used to be clay pipes tied on a twig. I remember one year we had snow, there was a shoot in the morning but I didn't go to it. It was the time there were a lot of those big French thrushes over. Big thrushes, they came when it was very cold, very fine, we hung nets between apple trees to catch them. No thrushes like that now and shags practically disappeared. We were not allowed to shoot seagulls, in the fog the captains could hear the seagulls and know they were close to land. We went out shooting cormorants when there was no fishing, we used to eat seagull eggs, they have a fishy taste.

'Big thrushes, I went out and we got hundreds, we had a chip basket full of birds to take home and I thought after this I would go to the shoot at the Pavilion. And of course there was always a few who'd had a few drinks, they asked, it was old Peg-Leg asked, where I'd been in the afternoon. I said, "If I'd come you wouldn't have won anything. There's a pipe there yet," I said, to hear him swear. . . . I couldn't do anything wrong that day. The gun was a bit hot, starting to kick a bit. I thought, "There'll be a bit of fun in a minute." I lent him my gun and it kicked at him, "It's not a gun you got," he said, "it's a cannon!" '

'I went to Sark as a baby, before the war, to see my grandmother. Then again in 1947. She had to rent a house, the Germans had taken her house down for firewood in the last winter of the Occupation, so she couldn't live at Clos de Dixcart, she had rented Dixcart Cottage opposite Dixcart Hotel. So, my first memories of Sark are Dixcart Cottage, the smell of meths reminds me because all the cooking was done on a meths cooker that campers use, you have to pump it up and light it with meths. I can remember taking a candle up to bed. It was still very formal, my grandparents dressed for dinner and the children were not seen, the tail end of another world. The children were rather intimidated. My grandparents were left over from the people who went to retire on Sark, they were not just middle-class, and they're not all middle-class now either, but they were people, gentry and a lot of them were not wealthy but had enough money to go and live there and saw the Sarkee as a peasant – not in a patronising way but as someone different. And they lived differently and they got servants if they could from amongst the Sarkese. And of course there weren't new houses being built to house the population, the sort of classless modern working population. The people who've gone to live on Sark now have built their own houses to do the various things that are done on the island in the way of commerce and so on. It was a different world.'

'The Belair had a dining room that was all mirrors and there were dances there. Very grand, you had to wait for the proprietors to take the floor first, all very good-looking.

'These days everything has changed. There are so many papers. Those involved in finance, oh, they have to have their papers. We had only *La Gazette* and that was weekly.'

'The Jonquiere – the green bed – always to be seen in the kitchen of an old Sark house. The corner is boxed in to make a large bed then boarded over and covered in green baize. Under the bed, in the box as it were, the furze is stored all ready chopped for the fire. When the men come in from the fields, or after a meal, they lie on the bed and rest, a hard bed for people who live hard. If anyone comes in with news or gossip, they sit on the green bed and we all gather round. There's no newspapers in Sark but the green bed doesn't miss much local news.'
  (FRANCIS DILLON, BBC Radio documentary, 1938)

Such is life in Sark. All the controversial topics of the day of the world at large do not worry these islanders, who are content to live as their fathers and forefathers have done. They have no ambition to see the outside world and theirs is indeed a peaceful existence.
  (CAPTAIN ERNEST PLATT, *Sark as I found it*)

The daily newspapers, they fill us with wonder and awe (is it possible? is it happening?), also with sickness and despair. The fixes, the scandals, the insanity, the idiocy, the piety, the lies, the noise. . . . Recently in *Commentary*, Benjamin DeMott wrote that the 'deeply lodged suspicion of the times is namely, that events and individuals are unreal, and that power to alter the course of the age, of my life and your life, is actually vested nowhere'. There seems to be, said DeMott, a kind of 'universal descent into unreality'. The other night – to give a benign example of the descent – my wife turned on the radio and heard the announcer offering a series of cash prizes for the three best television plays of five minutes' duration, written by children. It is difficult at such moments to find one's way around the kitchen. Certainly few days go by when incidents far less benign fail to remind us of what DeMott is talking about. When Edmund Wilson says that after reading *Life* magazine he feels he does not belong to the country depicted there, that he does not live in this country, I understand what he means.

(PHILIP ROTH, Writing American Fiction)

'Before the war everybody was quite happy with what they were doing. We never knew any better but unfortunately the majority of the people have seen the wide world and see how it is progressing and the twentieth century's caught up with us. They all want to move with the twentieth century. They never know what they're missing by going so fast.'

'There's lots of things we know about and see that we never knew before, it's made the world smaller. Everybody could play the piano, accordion, mouth organ. The old people used to tell stories and keep you occupied in the evening, sing songs and play cards. It's easier to switch on, very few people play the piano today.'

That night, a Friday, we gathered in front of the set, as was the custom and the rule, with take-out Chinese. There were floods, earthquakes, mud slides, erupting volcanoes. We'd never before been so attentive to our duty, our Friday assembly. Heinrich was not sullen, I was not bored. Steffie, brought close to tears by a sitcom husband arguing with his wife, appeared totally absorbed in these documentary clips of calamity and death. Babette tried to switch to a comedy series about a group of racially mixed kids who build their own communications satellite. She was startled by the force of our objection. We were otherwise silent, watching houses slide into the ocean, whole villages crackle and ignite in a mass of advancing lava. Every disaster made us wish for more, for something bigger, grander, more sweeping.

(DON DELILO, *White Noise*)

'Television. I remember the man first bought it. He was told it wouldn't go without electricity, he then agreed to have one light in the television room. The reception was very bad.'

The attraction of T.V. is insidious. Will there be a readjustment of social habits? Shall we become incapable of creating our own diversions? Shall we become lazy-minded, taking our entertainment and ideas automatically from the screen?

(JOHN SWIFT, *Adventures in Vision*)

'Electricity takes the sheer back-breaking drudgery out of life, television then simply caputs your mind and turns you into a vegetable. Television to me is almost the end of culture, what the world meant in the past, it means you go from free-thinking people into programmed zombies. There's always been that tendency but I think without such a potent medium to mould your thoughts people have had to think things out for themselves however inept they were at it but with television no thought is required ever again.'

'[They say] television is just another name for junk mail. But I tell them I can't accept that. I tell them I've been sitting in this room for more than two months, watching TV into the early hours, listening carefully, taking notes. A great and humbling experience, let me tell you. Close to mystical.'

'What's your conclusion?'

He crossed his legs primly and sat with the cup in his lap, smiling straight ahead.

'Waves and radiation,' he said. 'I've come to understand that the medium is a primal force in the American home. Sealed-off, timeless, self-contained, self-referring. It's like a myth being born right there in our living room, like something we know in a dream-like and preconscious way. I'm very enthused, Jack.'

(DON DELILO, *White Noise*)

Electricity came to the island [Iona] 32 years ago . . . and now one of the shops sells videos; Macinnes believes that television has killed off serious reading on the island, and his wife Ruth bemoans the passing of highland musical evenings in homes too.

(ANDREW STEPHEN, *Observer Magazine*, article on Iona, 1988)

Isolated examples, stories, old photographs and postcards, disagreements break out over the details, but this is – 'I'll tell you a story' – how things were on Sark. Images from the past, well worn, comfortable and comforting, explained to children who will sit still long enough to listen, taken out from the backs of old drawers, from the cache behind the clock on the mantelpiece, evidence pressed into the hands of impressionable outsiders:

'All this playschool is quite new, what I can remember is having to help in the house. Washing day was always Monday. Washing day we had an open fire outside with two iron bars across it and burnt gorse and sticks underneath with a copper on top. We used to put our sheets to dry on the common and our table cloths on the gorse. My mother took in washing and there were hampers of it, starch. . . . One iron warming while you used the other. Then we had a self-heating iron on a brick.

'I used to have to clean my room and grannie's. We had a Swift, the first washing machine, what you'd call a dolly with a wooden handle in a galvanised bucket. On a nice day like this one or two of us might go for a walk.'

*

'In the old days fishing there were not as many pots. Willow pots and then we got wet fish, whiting and put down lines. Before engines they sailed and rowed.

'That container that went down off the cargo boat last winter, it heeled over so fast it was very fortunate another didn't go. It's a bad boat. The engines are not powerful enough to go against the current. She can't take a wind above force 4. Scrap her this year they say, they should have kept to the old way, darned lazy, all the trailers on the Harbour Hill. . . . We had no baker, and no butcher's shop, meat and bread all came from Guernsey at one time and when it was rough the boat came in the bays, Havre Gosselin when the wind was in the east, Grand Grève or Eperquerie when in the south. A sack of bread on your back . . . one chap, a wonder he didn't kill himself, could bring up a quarter of beef.'

'We did all our own things, or that's what we think now. We had to make our own fun. Go to different places, go in crowds, our play was different. Children these days expect a lot more and they're better-off financially. Take Christmas. It was not what you would like. You had your stocking, stocking not a pillow case. A Christmas tree . . . I remember getting a green piece of material under the tree, cloth to make a new dress. We had oranges at Christmas. There were three girls in our family and our birthdays fell September, October and November. Each girl had a party every third year with her name on top of the cake.'

'Old people, I've met them and spoken to them but that's about all. There's no time when the whole island gets together, hardly anybody goes to church, there's only about four a week.'

'They were much more a knit family than they are now. I think they never will be other than always standing by one another but in those days they so depended on each other, utterly dependent on each other. That's the difference, it's not so much now. The young people on Sark now are growing up without any idea of what Sark was when their parents were young, no idea at all.'

'I was five when we went to Sark twelve days after the end of the Occupation. I can only assume my father was waiting to go. Maseline Harbour was built in 1949, I used to go and watch it, it was built by a well known diver, I watched him putting the concrete piles in. The harbour was an ugly thing, it became like the Pompidou Centre on Sark.

'I had carte blanche. I remember walking my friends back to Little Sark after the cinema, all the way up and the winds would be going across Grand Grève. Will Hay, *Tarzan*, *Fabian of the Yard*, Laurel and Hardy, and Deanna Durbin who I fell in love with and couldn't get over for five years. The cinema was in the Island Hall at seven in the evening, rain on the corrugated iron roof. I remember X when I asked him what the film was like he always said: "I don't know but I've heard it's supposed to be good. And the bloke that told me it's supposed to be good I always believed him. So, if he says it's supposed to be good I reckon I can say in all fairness it's supposed to be good." Every week he said that for several years.

'Sark had everything; the wild beaches, the valleys of the Congo, historic allusions to Napoleon with the cannons on the cliffs, blown trees. . . .'

Journalists visit the school but it's the school they want to capture, not the children. Documentary makers avoid them, the future of Sark is insignificant, the punters want the past.

'I'd like something for the children. You go to the pub, you can't get to the pool table because all the others are on it, the Island Hall is not the greatest of places, we have the Youth Club there, I mean it's quiet. . . . There's nothing really for the children. It doesn't bother me now because I'm used to it. If the children gave you a guided tour of what the island does for them it would be over in ten minutes. This island is aimed at adults and tourists, not really a children's island. You probably wouldn't notice it because you're an adult. If you can name something that's specifically for children I'd be glad to hear it. Apart from school there is nothing that is children only.'

'It's not like a village because it's more difficult to get off. Everything's closed here by about seven at the most, people in Guernsey, they hang around the fish and chip shop. It's not a place for people who depend on machines, space invaders, not a chance, or for those who need a coffee bar. There are discos mainly for the older ones. You can stand at the bar waiting to get a soft drink for absolutely ages. It's four to fifty, anyone can go to the disco as long as they're not barred from the pub. You're allowed light stuff at sixteen, heavy stuff at eighteen. It's such a small island you know how old everyone is. Visitors get away with it quite a lot but really the children over here, they just don't ask for strong drink, for a start it doesn't appeal to them and they know they won't get it anyway.'

'It's nice in the winter but it's so dead. You go up the village and nobody's there, at least in the summer, although you go mad with everybody ringing their bells and running everybody over. It's nice to see it busy, eh? You have to have tourists to survive but we should have less tourists doing more good.

'We get friends from the staff at hotels, make friends. If they don't like their job this summer or they lose it they won't come back, and it's usually the ones you make friends with who don't come back. I like going to Guernsey on a holiday but when you see some of the children over there you don't. I'm glad I'm not there.'

'My favourite place is somewhere on the cliffs, all on my own and it's nice and peaceful. Winter is brill. I like going up to Grève de la Ville, on the common, and standing there looking out and the wind's blowing straight in your face but it's lovely. I love doing that, getting blown about, it's good fun, isn't it?'

\*

'I'm nine. I've lived here nine years but I was born on Guernsey because there isn't a hospital over here. My dad's from Liverpool and my mum comes from Dorset. I think I would like to stay in Sark but I don't know. I don't think I miss football, we can play football in the Seigneur's field. I lead a different life from my cousins because there's no cars on Sark. I play pool and I come to the youth club every week. It's ten pence an hour, more boys than girls come.'

'The harbour is the best place, busier than most places, I like looking at the boats. I work in the summer. I'm fourteen and I get £1.50 an hour, my cousin in England is sixteen and she's getting £1.45. I make sure the trays are ready with the cutlery and the saucers, I go and wipe the tables down outside and when that's done I wipe all the tables in the kitchen. Get the knives and forks out. I work for something to do, in England people can go down to the town and mooch around the shops, you can't do that over here.'

'I'm fifteen and I'm leaving school. My father is happy for me to stay around. I want to stay here, this is my home, the place I'm used to, all my family are here, this is all I want, I don't want to change my life.

'My dad's a fisherman and he's the Prévot and my mum's a housewife, that keeps me fed. I've always got jobs on the farm or fishing. We sell as much fish here as we can but the rest goes to Guernsey. Only two hotels support the farmers, Dixcart and Stocks. On our farm our main product, apart from milk and butter, we do maize for the cows, carrots and other things to sell, potatoes. We keep a lot for ourselves really because during the winter we move into one house – my aunt and uncle, my two cousins and my family.

'Round Christmas we move into Gran and Pop's, make a nice Christmas spirit for the three weeks of Christmas, that's what I enjoy most, about twelve of us down there.

'The fishing season is from April 1st to the end of October. Then my father repairs the fishing boat, does carpentry or works on the farm. In last year's hurricane we lost our fishing boat. The boat was at Les Laches, our mooring was too strong, the boat couldn't take the weight so it broke. I woke up at about half past five because they were shouting. The first thing I remember all the power lines were down so there was no light. Dad had just had a call to say the boat had vanished. Some had gone down to check on their boats at the harbour at about 4 a.m. Dad and my brother went down and while they were there I went to check on the livestock down on the farm, everything was soaked down there. When my brother came back we started to clear up the roads. There were trees on the road. Then I went to school and eventually I learnt that the boat had gone. There was hope that we'd be able to find it on a beach somewhere but it was smashed. We found a new boat in Weymouth when we were on holiday last year and that's the boat we've got now. The hurricane just came and went, there was no warning and I slept through it. A tree fell on one of the power lines down at the Mermaid so that was all that corner of the island cut off.'

'Summer seems short and winter seems very long. I've got my selection of models to make from Guernsey, boats and planes. This year I even made a cake for the Produce Show. Easter holidays is the start of the season but as soon as the kids go back to school then the parents stop coming. It's nice to have the island back to yourself without thousands of visitors crawling around the place but in the summer it's nice as well because you see new people.'

'Everyone knows each other, in ways I like it but in other ways I don't. Say if you take this latest thing. I was told to keep it hush hush on Sunday and then I hear it from someone else on Monday! Everybody knows your business, that really annoys me. No, they don't help, they rub your nose in it more, "Oh look what they've done!" Generally people stick together. You can tell somebody one thing in Little Sark and it will be right round the island by next morning, you can guarantee it.'

*

'I wanted to stay but I don't know now that I . . . this may sound really funny . . . but now that I'm a teenager everything's sort of . . . really changed. I see everything in a different way, it's a new world now, grown-up now. Everything seems so different now, taking all the things more seriously when I used to take them all without a care. Friends come but they don't live here, they turn up out of the blue and then go back again.'

'There are a lot of children born now, well half of them are Sark and half English – islanders. But as they're not born here, they're not really Sark. It is where you're born you get the nationality. They're born on Guernsey now, they're Guernseyites, no matter what they say.'

'. . . all the more they remember their forebears. Islands are the home of genealogies. . . . In the Channel Islands, relationships are venerated.
(VICTOR HUGO, *L'Archipel de la Manche*)

'I'm nine, I've lived in Guernsey for half a year with my dad and then I came over to Sark when I was half a year old and I love it here. I love youth club and school, rounders and things like that. Old Philip is my uncle, young Philip's my cousin. I'm very proud of my uncle and my family. I go with Mum on the carriage and I feed the pigs and I clean the pigs out when Nanna hasn't got anyone to work for her. I go riding.

'I won't leave Sark because I've got a place to get a job, I think, on a farm or on a boat. I go out with my step-dad a lot in the boat and my dad's got a boat and my grandpa's got a yacht and a cargo ship. I don't get fed up in the winter, it's good fun going down Happy Valley when it's snowing on a toboggan. I don't mind about shops because I've got enough things already. In the summer I go swimming down at the harbour, I learnt to swim when I was six, it took me two days. I'm a good diver now, my step-dad is a good diver you see and he has a fishing boat and he gets ormers and he goes out in his boat fishing and he's a diver as well. He bought some ormers from a special aquarium, they are little ones that are 18p each and he'll sell them when they're grown. I'm interested in power boats and so is my cousin. I don't miss driving a car because I'll drive a tractor, my mum's a speed freak on a tractor.'

'England was very crowded and I'm glad to be here. I want to be a hairdresser.'

# Epilogue

May 1989. 7.30 a.m. Eastleigh airport no longer shed-fringed, more like a bomb site now. Upstairs in the terminal fried breakfasts, summer suits, smokers get one in before the check-in. Children buying sweets, parents swing the book stand – *I Ching*, *23 Steps to Success and Achievement, Star Signs, Develop Your ESP, Success Through a Positive Mental Attitude.* Slogan t-shirts and key rings, 'I've been Heducated', horribly colourful soft toys.

Women look after children, men read newspapers, 'It's Tough Clough'. Watch luggage being hurled onto a truck beyond the glass doors, a Scottie dog goes out in a cage, a wheelchair goes out to a plane. Hostesses for once not shivering in their poly-cotton uniforms. *Daily Mail,* 'Long Blast from the Kremlin', business-man with briefcase on his knee, the slimmer the briefcase the better, businessmen the modern Masai, a briefcase slim enough for a blue video.

On the plane and the hostesses in short white gloves (the ankle sock of the hand) close cabin baggage holders with a snap. The Scottie barks, the Masai remove their jackets, very carefully. The Captain sounds like a DJ, 'Talk to you again shortly', fails to tell us his star sign.

Hostesses go through the lifejacket routine sub-Victoria Wood: 'This is the whistle for attracting attention. Don't inflate the lifejacket till out of the aircraft as this may impede your exit.'

For the first time I meet no Sark people at either airport. The Queen on Guernsey today will be on Sark tomorrow, Sark will be closed for the day, perhaps everybody has stayed at home? Look about for familiar faces, recognise the Scottie first off the luggage carousel.

The quay for the Sark boat has been changed, perhaps because of the arrival of *Britannia*. Half an hour before the boat sails and the quay is already swimming in Courtelle cardigans, support hose, hundreds queuing, yellow badges, a pile of leaflets in the Sark Shipping Office, *Discover Sark*. To the right of the queue a different sort of chap altogether is helping out two holidaymakers who will be staying in one of Sark's best hotels. Everything about him, height, shoes, clothes, authority . . . Englishness. Only his wife seems unimpressed, sulking. 'About fifteen of us on Little Sark,' he says. 'Sark is quite different, it's the absence of well . . . everything.'

The boat has a new sign, 'Passengers in a drunken state will not be carried'. Meet a young man vaguely related to the late Dame. I draw the complicated tree in my notebook before realising how quickly one loses perspective, how this is of limited interest to virtually everyone. As I disembark I say hello to an old Sarkee whose company I cherished in the winter. As he smiles I realise he doesn't recognise me.

On Sark, flowers upon flowers, the smell of wild white lupins that make you stop, turn and go back. The harbour looks unusually smart, the railings newly painted. The tea cabin has had to be moved, hear a grumble about this straight away. Flags outside the Electricity Supply Company, flags across the Avenue. An old man I spoke with last summer has died, his house has been levelled, cleared, gravelled and now has two benches on it. One wonders, looking at it – everything that went on in that house, quite flattened. He lived in this narrow space for over seventy years, he died in the doorway, he left a gravelled gap.

The field at the old man's house has not been used for sheep or horses over the winter. A meadow now that the matrons of Camden would cherish, a meadow in which to advertise margarine. The pebble in the palm still haunts me, what you might know about a tiny place like Sark is never-ending. Friends tell me of a botanist now staying at the Hivernage who says that the Rose Bay Willow Herb only came to Sark five years ago. The botanist is a shy man with a deaf aid in each ear. . . .

The old man, the oldest man on the island, is going to be

presented to the Queen tomorrow and jokes about it as he passes on his way to the village. He's annoyed that he'll not be allowed to take photographs of her when he is presented in the Island Hall but his family are coming over from Guernsey, they'll take a video of him as he comes out. I stand on my own in his meadow and think, the Pilcher Monument a finger of stone in a tiny mown field which goes out to the point. Cuckoos, pigeons, tractors, the window open at the old man's house, his wife in dreams crosses the field to kiss him and say sorry.

At 7 a.m. on the day of Juliet's command performance the dirt roads in the centre of the village are being hosed down to stop the dust and the man who owns most of the shops on the Avenue is cutting down weeds with ferocity. There is no litter in any of the bins. The secret service are here already, so they say. Small places make even the most innocent behaviour look suspicious, I feel suspicious looking in the bins. The Vicar, unsuspicious and this morning very smart, sits outside his locked church waiting for a security visit.

No one is serving coffee today. Conversation in the shops revolves on where best to stand for the view and the photograph. French holidaymakers – suspected of revolutionary zeal? – are told they are not allowed to run or to bicycle when the Queen's carriages are going past. Stand for an hour in one shop and talk, again, about the truth of what happened during the Occupation. Ignoring the Marxist broom I buy a dozen reproduction postcards – the mill with a Zeppelin floating above it, the Coupée before the Germans concreted it and added rails, rowing boats and lobster pots stacked against the cliffs at Le Creux – and three exorbitantly expensive Sark memorial Queen's Visit mugs.

The Queen is due to land at Maseline Harbour at 3.00, at 2.25 it's already 80 in the shade and the British Legion, lined up against the graveyard wall for her inspection, cast long shadows. On the little island of grass around the Cenotaph are the press, pink badges, 'Royal Visit', clip-boards, self-importance, gods who talk exclusively to one another; their grey and furry outside broadcast mikes lie like corgis at their feet.

A hundred yards from the church, the Island Hall, lilies in stone tubs, yards of bunting. All the quarantine tenants have been invited here to meet the Queen, some arrive on foot, others in carriages, some in medals, all the women in hats. I ask a tenant I have never seen before whether one of the old Sarkee tenants has arrived yet, she's never met him, doesn't know who he is.

The bell tolls at the church, the Queen is late and by 3.12 the British Legion line-up wilts. A child with an unopened bottle of squash in his lap cries in a pushchair in the shade, two other children scuff their sandals in the dust. At last eight carriages bring the Queen and her entourage. No jumping up and down or flag waving but restrained clapping, no crash barriers here, no pushing or shoving, ordinary mortals get as fine a look-in – for photographs is what it's all about – as the press.

The Queen signs the visitor's book in the church, then gets back into her carriage to be driven down to the new medical centre. Cameras click, Prince Philip makes a joke or two, a man beside me in the crowd points out the Home Secretary, Douglas Hurd.

The god-like press not covering the opening of the island medical centre – the moving of the little curtain which somehow always reminds me of a cremation – preen in the sunshine. An exotic-looking woman in spotted jersey trousers that narrow on a slim ankle runs a hand – no honest toil about it – through her long blonde hair. 'Who are you representing? My feet are killing me.' The sound of clapping, the smell of honeysuckle in the hedge.

Thirty-four men on the island have been sworn in as special constables for the day, everybody's brothers, husbands and friends like parish priests in Ireland. Two policemen have come across from Guernsey, proper uniforms, helmets, white gloves. They beam at the gathering crowd and look generally benevolent, unpoliticised police, the sort who see you across a road, wipe down children's lollies with clean hankies, the sort who appear in Agatha Christie stories and are patronised by detective inspectors. By contrast the plain-clothes security chief looks professional, preoccupied. He has the face and body of something from the wardrobe department, stroppy and firm, stocky and close-shaven, compressed like a spring in a badly cut grey suit.

Back walks the Queen and her entourage, shaking hands, asking questions, then disappears once more, into the Island Hall where the quarantine tenants, Sark's dignitaries and the old man wait.

'They're getting wine and sherry,' someone tells me. 'The Queen is lovely, isn't she, but the Queen Mum she's a sweetie.' A young American in startling earrings negotiates the possibility, perhaps it is the concept, of buying a policeman's helmet. The Guernsey policeman is all jokes and flattery and much talk of the American coming over to the police station in Guernsey the next day. Chief security remains sombre with eyes in the back of his head, shifting people till he likes what he sees – 'I don't trust anyone. Ask my wife.' He is all eyebrows and stomach and mops his brow with a large male handkerchief, moves on a woman with flowering garlic in her hair and another with a small plastic Union Jack stuck into the plaster cast on her arm. 'I live here fifty-two weeks of the year' cuts no ice with him. He is patently relieved when the Queen leaves the hall, settles into her carriage for the drive back down towards the harbour. As the crowd wanders off to Point Robert to see the last of the royal barge he loosens his tie, talks about the carriages: "I said what the hell are you polishing?" he said, "Everything I can bloody see." ' Guernsey policemen take their coats off, English women in Russell & Bromley shoes air their narrow feet. The children have got down to Coke and sandwiches laid out on tables along the Avenue. A tape recorder plays from the Da San Café, 'Nellie the Elephant', 'The Runaway Train', 'How Much is that Doggie in the Window?' A transistor in an open window talks of students mustering in Peking. 'It was just a skirt, top and a hat wasn't it?' says a little girl.

The weather is wonderful and I can't sleep. I cycle down to Little Sark and have coffee at 7.30 a.m. the next morning with a friend and an elderly Frenchman whose watch is wrong and hopes it's time for breakfast. At the old man's house it's business as usual, hanging out his sheets, the peg bag round his waist. I have the whole day ahead of me but I don't know what to do with it as it's a leaving day.

I wander about blankly, fritter away the time. I walk down to Le Vieux Port, through the farmyard and back through the valley, not a soul about. Down past La Fregondée cottages to stand above the sea at Havre Gosselin. Somewhere on the route I must have brushed past Giant Hogweed, both my arms have gone a funny colour above the elbow; only later does this begin to blister like a burn and hurt.

I feel like a stranger and I look like something escaped from the burns unit. I leave with the day trippers on the five o'clock boat. They're roaring with laughter because it's rough just outside the harbour, 'Weather must be on the change for it to be up like this', 'Shan't need a shower this evening'. Everyone, including grannies, looks very brown. 'It's the only place where you can lie down in a field and listen to silence,' someone says.

On the plane, arms akimbo, it's encouraging to be told by the doom merchant in the next seat that though the blisters on my skin will pop, eventually, the scars won't. Juliet answers back.

Back at Eastleigh the English tenement holder who didn't seem to know the others is waiting for her luggage. Resist the temptation to go over and talk to her, we'd hardly get beyond platitudes around the carousel. But I wonder what she's thinking as she lifts the suitcase which has her hat in it, the hat she wore just yesterday when she was presented as a feudal relic to the Queen.

Hurry across the bomb site to the car, roar past the last open filling station and then worry about running out of petrol and, ridiculously, of being raped if I have to walk to fetch a can.

Think of the old man, his cuckoo clock stuck at 9.40. Think of him watching himself in the video of the day he was presented to the Queen. Think of all the nights when he's alone and he swishes the kettle with his good hand, takes the cloth off the water jug in the back kitchen which used to be the dairy where he separated out the milk. Replacing the lid of the kettle with the little air duct at the back, 'That steam can burn you'. The square of greaseproof paper on the table with his cereal for tomorrow. A place for everything and everything in its place, binoculars, tide tables, *TV Times*.

# Bibliography

Barrell, John and Bull, John (eds), *The Penguin Book of Pastoral Verse*, Allen Lane, London, 1975.

Batchelor, John, *Mervyn Peake*, Gerald Duckworth, London, 1974.

Brody, Hugh, *Inishkillane: Change and Decline in the West of Ireland*, Allen Lane, London, 1973.

Cachemaille, J. L. V., *The Island of Sark 1874–5*, revised and edited by Laura E. Hale, London, 1928.

Calder-Marshall, Arthur, *The Innocent Eye: The Life of Robert J. Flaherty*, W. H. Allen, London, 1963.

Clark, Leonard, *Island of 100 Bays*, radio broadcast 1956, BBC Written Archives Centre.

DeLillo, Don, *White Noise*, Viking Penguin, London, 1985.

Dillon, Francis, *Welcome to Sark: A Radio Ecology*, 1938, BBC Written Archives Centre.

Edwards, G. B., *The Book of Ebenezer Le Page*, Hamish Hamilton, London, 1981

Ewen, A. H. and De Carteret, Allan R., *The Fief of Sark*, Guernsey Press, Guernsey, 1969.

Friel, Brian, *Making History*, Faber and Faber, London, 1989.

Fussell, Paul, *Abroad: British Literary Travelling Between the Wars*, Oxford University Press, Oxford, 1980.

Garnett, David, *Man in the Zoo and Lady into Fox*, Hogarth Press, London, 1982.

Gilmore, Maeve, *A World Away: A Memoir of Mervyn Peake*, Victor Gollancz, London, 1970.

Golding, William, *Lord of the Flies*, Faber and Faber, London, 1954.

Gordon, Lyndall, *Virginia Woolf: A Writer's Life*, Oxford University Press, Oxford, 1986.

Hammond, J. L. and Hammond, Barbara, *The Bleak Age*, Penguin Books, London, 1934.

Hardy, Thomas, *Tess of the d'Urbervilles*, Collins, London, 1974.

Hathaway, Sibyl, *Dame of Sark*, William Heinemann, London, 1961.

Heaney, Seamus, *Preoccupations: Selected Prose, 1968–78*, Faber and Faber, London, 1980.

*Household Words*, 20 October 1855.

Hugo, Victor *L'Archipel de la Manche/The Channel Islands*, La Haule Books, Jersey, 1988.

de Kadt, Emanuel, *Tourism: Passport to Development? – Perspectives on the Social and Cultural Effects of Tourism on Developing Countries*, Oxford University Press, Oxford, 1979.

Kavanagh, Patrick, 'The Great Hunger', from *The Complete Poems*, Goldsmith Press, Newbridge, Co. Kildare, 1986.

Kundera, Milan, *The Joke*, Faber and Faber, London, 1983.

LaTrobe, G. and L., *Scrambles on Sark: Guide to the Coast and Bays of Sark*, Guernsey, 1914.

MacNeice, Louis, *The Strings are False*, Faber and Faber, London, 1965.

Marshall, Michael, *Hitler Invaded Sark*, Guernsey Press, Guernsey, 1963.

'Old Customs of the Island of Sark', Radio Trek, 1946, radio broadcast, BBC Written Archives Centre.

Ondaatje, Michael, *Running in the Family*, Victor Gollancz, London, 1983.

Orme, Eve, *Sark Remembered*, radio broadcast for *Woman's Hour*, 1963, BBC Written Archives Centre.

Peake, Mervyn, *Mr Pye*, William Heinemann, London, 1953.

Platt, Captain Ernest, FRGS, *Sark as I found it*, John Laughton, London, 1935.

Robin, E. Gallienne, *Extremes Meet: A Song of Sark*, F. Clarke, States Arcade Guernsey, 1899.

Roth, Philip, extract from *Writing American Fiction*. (Reprinted with permission from *Reading Myself and Others*, Farrar, Straus and Giroux, 1975. Quoted in *The Novel Today*, Malcolm Bradbury, Fontana, London, 1977.)

Sacks, Oliver W., *The Man who Mistook his Wife for a Hat*, Gerald Duckworth, London, 1985.

Seaton-Wood, Alan and Seaton-Wood, Mary, *Islands in Danger*, Evans Brothers, London, 1955.

Sellar, W. C. and Yeatman, R. J., *1066 And All That*, Methuen, London, 1930.

Shayer, David, *Swinburne the Poet Visits Guernsey and Sark, 1876*, Toucan Press, Guernsey, 1980.

Smart, Borlaise, 'Sark: A New Artists' Colony', article in *The Artist*, November 1933.

Spark, Muriel, *The Girls of Slender Means*, Macmillan, London, 1963.

Steel, Tom, *The Life and Death of St Kilda*, Fontana, London, 1975.

Steinbeck, John, *Of Mice and Men*, William Heinemann, London, 1937.

Stephen, Andrew, 'Iona', article printed in *Observer Magazine*, 1988.

Stoney, Barbara, *Sibyl, Dame of Sark*, Hodder and Stoughton, London, 1978.

Swift, John, *Adventures in Vision*, John Lehmann, 1950.

Synge, J. M., *The Aran Islands*, Blackstaff Press, Belfast, 1988.

Terkel, Studs, *The Great Divide: Second Thoughts on the American Dream*, Hamish Hamilton, London, 1988.

Tremayne, Julia, *War on Sark: The Secret Letters of Julia Tremayne*, Webb and Bower, Exeter, 1981.

Watney, John, *Mervyn Peake*, Michael Joseph, London, 1976.

Williams, Raymond, *The Country and the City*, Chatto and Windus, London, 1973.

Williams, Raymond, *Keywords*, Fontana, London, 1976.

Winnington, G. Peter (ed.), *Peake Studies*, vol. 1, no. 1, Autumn 1988.